A LIFE IGNITED

IGNITE YOUR INNER FUSE

RHONDA KINARD

authorHOUSE®

AuthorHouse™
1663 Liberty Drive
Bloomington, IN 47403
www.authorhouse.com
Phone: 1 (800) 839-8640

Published by AuthorHouse   05/06/2016

ISBN: 978-1-5049-2015-5 (sc)
ISBN: 978-1-5049-2016-2 (hc)
ISBN: 978-1-5049-2014-8 (e)

Library of Congress Control Number: 2015910335

Print information available on the last page.

To my children, my amazing gifts from God:
Arnez Jr. and Lauren Tyler

You are my motivation and the joy of everything I do.
You are incredible little humans who embody the spirit of A
Life Ignited with every new adventure and new activity you
try. Continue to soak up knowledge, have fun, and laugh.
Enjoy life. You only live once.

I love you.

Mom

Contents

ACKNOWLEDGMENTS

NO WOMAN IS AN ISLAND. Just as it takes a village to raise a child, it also takes a village to write a book. Trust me; I did not do this alone. I stood safely on, around, and in the arms of people who love and supported me during the entire process of writing, publishing, and getting this book out to the world. And to these people, my village, I am grateful and thankful for the part each one of you played in helping me achieve a lifelong dream.

I thank God for my family, my friends, and my village. I thank God for allowing my vision of being a published author to become a reality. I get to share my stories, life lessons, and life experiences with the world for the purpose of helping others get through those seasons of uncertainty and rough patches in their lives. I thank God for the desire to serve people and the resilience to push forward despite the obstacles that try to defer my dreams. I thank God for the avidity to write and complete this book. I thank Him in advance for the people

I will meet, the lives this book will change, and the blessings this book will birth.

I owe so much to my husband, who requires so little of me. He's so patient with me. There were times I was working on this book when I was quite a handful to deal with. To say it plainly, he dealt with my crap and quietly stood in the gap; being that rock and foundation that I've grown to rely on as a source of calm and security. Thank you, Arnez, for loving me without judgment or expectation. You are my first and only true love, and my very best friend. We've been riding together for more than twenty years now, for richer and poorer, in sickness and in health, and I couldn't imagine the thrill of this roller-coaster ride with anyone else. Thank you for believing in me and encouraging me to write this book. Thank you for continually being a shoulder to lean, cry, and laugh on. Thank you for being you. I can do what I do because of your love, dedication to my dreams, and financial support. Thank you for your patience and for holding down our family and our household when I needed those extra few hours to sit up in the office and write. And thank you for those many nights when I was deliriously tired where you just ignored my mood swings and loved me through my craziness. I appreciate you and thank you for being my friend. I love you.

To Arnez Jr., my firstborn and only son: You are my "cut-the-fool" buddy. We share some of the funniest times together. You and I have the same silly sense of humor. I love when we laugh, dance, and start busting on one another. I love that you laugh at my jokes, even when they are not remotely funny. I never imagined I'd have such a fun relationship with my son. Our relationship is special and important to me. Even in your youth, you get me. You try to understand your Mom and I appreciate that. Thank you for believing in me and for offering your support every step of the way. Thank you for your smiles, jokes, and the moments when we danced, tried to harmonize, or acted super silly with one another. Those moments helped relax me at times when I felt a bit overwhelmed. Thank you for your concern. You would always ask, "Mom, how's the book coming along?" I love you for always checking in and making sure I was okay. You are an amazing young man. I am honored and blessed to travel on this journey with such an incredible son by my side. I love you.

To my beautiful daughter Lauren Tyler: My "Lovie". You danced, sang, and tumbled in the office while I was writing because you wanted to keep me company. You wanted me to feel that someone was always there with me. You were always eager to help me, and for that, I love you so much. Thank you for believing in *A Life Ignited*. Your love and support mean so much to me. Your creativity keeps my imaginative juices flowing. I love how hard you work and the way you commit yourself 100% to your goals. You are so much like me in that way. You're quite the firecracker. I know you are going to set this world on fire with your many talents and gifts. I'm going to be right there with you—along for the ride. I'll support and encourage you the same way you have supported and encouraged me. You're a rock star, Lauren Tyler. I love you.

To my mom, the incredibly awesome Cynthia Coleman: Thank you for helping me with *A Life Ignited* from the very beginning. You went with me to my very first event, and you were with me when I met my first high-profile client. Thank you for being an unwavering example of a strong, yet gentle, courageous, kind, and faithful woman. Thank you for teaching me how to be a good person. Thank you for praying for me. Thank you for being my friend. And even though you are my friend, I am quite aware that you are Mom first – "Don't let the smooth taste fool ya'!" I love you, Mom.

To my friend Marrea Walker-Smith: I am so glad our paths crossed. We connected instantly. Thank you for your friendship and wisdom. Our conversations give me good laughs when I need them most. Good friends make you better, stronger, and more confident about the possibilities of life. And you are definitely my good friend. I look up to you and respect you for all you've accomplished. I appreciate you, dear friend.

To my corporate-America work friends, Don Tinneny and James Ware (like how I classified you guys?): You are the two people who make working in an office fun. The three of us have similar dreams and interests, and it was always a great day when we got together to share our stories about our kids, spouses, vacations, and life in general. Thanks for the giggles, laughs, and jokes. You guys are awesome men with really cute kids, and I pray that you have success and prosperity beyond your wildest dreams.

To all the artists who shared their creative gifts with me at the photo shoot for the book cover: Words cannot express my gratitude to Devonna Randolph of Devonna's Hair Design, Bobbi Innocenzo of Bella Angel for her gift of make-up artistry, Laura Eaton of Laura Eaton Photography for the beautiful photos and her attention to detail, and Nicolette Wilson of Change Consultant Solutions for being the most professional, enthusiastic, and efficient personal concierge I have ever worked with. Thank you for being a part of my special day.

The photo shoot was so much fun. The day would not have been the same without each of you there.

I want to give one big thank you to everyone who supports and contributes to *A Life Ignited*. I thank God for you, and I will never forget the support and love you have shown me.

INTRODUCTION

Be not afraid of life. Believe that life is worth living,
and your belief will help create the fact.
—William James

HOW EXTRAORDINARY WOULD YOUR LIFE be if you stood
in your power, walked in your purpose, pursued
your passion unapologetically, and soared toward the greater
success, fulfillment, and happiness in life you crave? Think
about what your life would look like if you were reaching your
goals and crushing obstacles in your way. Envision yourself
being radiant and unstoppable, like a firework exploding in
the night sky, as you soar toward all you want to achieve and
accomplish. What would you be doing if you thought you
could not fail? How would you present your best and most
brilliant self to the world, and live your best life? Imagine being
so fierce and powerful that nothing could stand in the way of

your passion or your purpose? Take a few moments, close your eyes, and luxuriate in the vision you have for your life. What will your life look like when you expose your greatness within, reach your goals, and accomplish your dreams?

> *What does that picture look like?*
> *What do you look like?*
> *What are you doing?*
> *Where are you?*
> *How do you feel?*
> *Who is there with you and what are they doing?*
> *How do they feel?*

Believe right now, in this moment, that this vision you have for your life can be your reality! With passion, determination, and the 'right' actions, you can live the life you crave. You don't have to just sit on the sidelines and watch other people live the life you want and do the things you want to do, or be what you desire to be. You can have the life you crave. You can be the things you want to be. You can serve the people you want to serve. Regardless of what it looks like right now, you have the power to get out of the situation you are in and make your life great again. Growing up in a home where the bills barely got paid, and heat and hot water were a luxury, trust me when I tell you, if you believe that your current circumstance does not define your final destination, you can absolutely, without a doubt, rise above where you are, and live in abundance and peace, with good health, prosperity, and happiness in tow. If your mind can conceive it, you can work to achieve it. Declare that you can and will achieve firework status in your life. Claim it today! Speak it into existence. Say it boldly and truly believe, "I AM A LIFE IGNITED!"

It's time for you to quit holding back your greatness. Behind the many walls you've built, you are explosive. You are ready to soar towards all that you want and know that you need in life. This book will help you identify the walls and roadblocks standing in your way, and support you as you move forward with a new mind-set and a clearer picture of what you need to do to reach your goals and live your life ignited. Everything you need to be great is within you. I know in times of weakness it's hard to believe that the power to change your life lies with you, but it does. You just haven't tapped into your greatness yet - or you've let your greatness lay unused and immobilized for so long that you've forgotten the force to be reckoned with that you really are. This book will encourage and motivate you to break down barriers, create opportunities, and believe in the brilliance you possess to make your vision a reality and live your life ignited.

You are the answer to the perceived problems in your life. You hold the key to unlock the door to your success. You are the ladder. You are the bridge. YOU are the solution. And as you read about the different strategies and solutions in this book, I want you to remember that no one else can take action for you. No one else can get you where you want and need to be. You have to be willing to do the work, open your mind to different ways of thinking, and be purposeful as you move forward and apply these strategies, solutions, and practices to your life.

Many people know they have yet to scratch the surface of their fullest potential. They know they are not walking in their purpose. They are unhappy, unfulfilled, and settling for less than the best they can give to themselves and their families. They are sick and tired of being sick and tired and they are ready for a change. Can you relate to any of this? Many people will find their way to this book in search of answers, clues, and motivation to go from just surviving and dealing with circumstances to thriving and creating their own success and happiness in life. They are looking to fill the void, and bridge the gap from mediocre and mundane to amazing and living "A Life Ignited".

I wrote this book because I want to meet you in that gap. I will motivate and inspire you to cross over from a life where you are not activating your super powers, walking in your purpose, and living your best life to a life where you give yourself permission to stand in your power, follow your dreams, and allow confidence and faith to lead you towards all that you crave in life.

The reason many people are not living the lifestyle they desire is because they are stuck in a R.U.T. and have allowed self-doubt and fear to convince them into believing they're not worthy, capable or equipped with the tools and resources needed to live the life they envision for themselves. I get it! I've been the victim of RUT's, too. So many opportunities passed me by because I was too afraid to own my awesome sauce, too worried about other people's opinions, intimidated by the unknown, and scared to be my authentic self because I wanted to fit in and wanted people to like me.

As a kid, I had a secret infatuation with country music and line dancing. But I was a little brown girl from the hood. My friends would have called me all

*sorts of names, like corny and weird, if I told them I
loved country music and country line dancing, so I
pretended to only love hip-hop and R&B. Later in life,
I realized that being weird and corny were a few of my
superpowers and assets that served me well in life.*

*As adults, how many people are still suppressing
their truest selves worried that if they show people who
they really are, people will not like them? When you de-
value yourself for the sake of wanting others to like you,
YOU disrespect and discredit your very own authenticity
(your unique blend of personality, talents, and gifts) and
prevent yourself from experiencing the greatness that
only you can exude and deliver to the world!*

The reason I started coaching as a profession is because I
have a natural desire to help people overcome "mind-grenades".
That's a term I made up that refers to the lies we tell ourselves
that we start to believe, that ultimately keep us from walking in
purpose and prosperity. You've probably allowed a few of these
mind-grenades to blow up in your mind and wreak havoc on
your confidence a time or two. Mind-grenades destroy your
ability to move forward with your goals and dreams. Some
common mind-grenades you may have struggled with are:

- I can't
- I'm not ready
- What if I fail?
- No one will buy it
- I don't have enough money

- I'm too fat
- What if they say no?
- People will look at me funny
- I have to act this way if I want them to like me
- No one likes me
- Who will buy anything from me?
- Who am I? I'm not worthy
- This isn't so bad. It can always be worse
- I don't have resources
- I don't know where to start
- I'm scared to fail
- I'm scared to succeed

This book will help you destroy mind-grenades before they detonate. I will help you unlearn the unhealthy and unproductive patterns of mediocrity that all originated from mind-grenades that you let erupt in your mind. Because I've been there, done that, and sabotaged my own success and happiness with mind-grenades, I can totally relate to how these mind-grenades play tricks on your emotions and your ability to be unstoppable and uncompromising as you work towards your goals and dreams. I want you to know you are not alone. You are not on this journey by yourself. Your feelings and mind-grenades are not isolated and unique to you. Anyone who has ever attempted to pursue greatness, step out of the box, and break family curses has had these same feelings, but the difference between those who successfully reach goals and live happy lives and those who are still stuck in their RUT's is that although successful people have mind-grenades, they do not allow them to destroy their passion and the vision for what they desire. Your desire to live your life ignited has to be bigger and stronger than your mind-grenades.

You are very powerful, provided you know how
powerful you are.
- Yogi Bhajan

In this book, I share intimate episodes from my life where I was faced with various challenges and mind-grenades. I share with you how I was able to pursue my passion with purpose and live a life ignited – an abundantly blessed life that I am proud of, despite the many blasts that went off in my head and held me back from living in my fullest potential for so long. I teach, motivate, and inspire you to overcome mind-grenades so you can live a more fulfilled and happy life by sharing tips, advice, and my very own personal reflections on how to reach your goals, love yourself more, and pursue the vision you have for your life no matter what. I help you get out of your own way so that you can begin to live the life ignited you desire, deserve, and crave.

There is something you are not satisfied with or
happy about. You know you are not operating on a full
tank of potential right now. You know you could do
better and you crave a life that reflects what you know
you are capable of achieving. You want this thing so
very bad. Your purpose calls you, but you don't answer
the call. The doctor told you to change your diet or risk
disease or death, but you refrain from making the dietary
changes required to save your own life. You know you

*are in a toxic relationship, but you are too afraid to
leave. You stay in your cozy comfort zone because your
friends are there and they accept you as you are. You
want to grow your business, but you are not committed
or consistent. You have relationship goals, but you berate
and blame the other person and always feel you need
to win the arguments. Your financial mind-set keeps
you from moving forward with your future plans, and
you keep spending money, you don't have, on frivolous
things you don't need. You want to go back to school so
that you can increase your earning potential at work,
but you won't plan and prioritize and you continue to
procrastinate. You want to look better and lose weight,
but you never refuse the cookies and donuts and rarely
go to the gym or workout. You want to be a more positive
person, but you hang around negative people. It's time to
get positioned with your purpose and start living the life
you are capable of living.*

*No more excuses! No more settling! No more fear!
It's time to start living Your Life Ignited.*

Before we move forward, it's important to understand what
I mean by a RUT (an Ignited term). At this point, I've used
the term a few times. A RUT is a "Really Unproductive Time
(or Place)" in your life. The U in the acronym RUT can also
stand for:

- unhealthy
- unhappy

- unmotivated
- unacceptable
- unfulfilling

Why do people stay in a RUT for so long? Why do we stay in unhealthy relationships when we know we should have and deserve better? Why do we continue to go back and forth to jobs that bring us more sadness than joy? Why do we eat health-unfriendly foods and live sedentary lifestyles, knowing that our doctors warned us about diabetes and hypertension? Why do we continue to rely on people who cannot keep their own heads above water, yet we expect them to help us elevate and advance our purposes? Why do we allow mediocre people, places, and things to keep us down when we desire so much more? Well, because RUT's thrive on one thing – a lack of power. When you relinquish your energy to some person or thing that hurt you or to a mind-grenade that exploded in your head, you become more and more powerless. The moment the diet failed, the relationship failed, the person at work disappointed you, you didn't get that raise, you stopped writing the book, you dropped out of school, or you got scared or intimidated by the climb, and you quit trying, you gave up power. When you got knocked down and stayed down, you became powerless. And when you decided to stay down for a long period of time, you found yourself in a RUT – feeling powerless over what you let crush your confidence and defeat you. When you're in a RUT, you feel helpless over the problems you're facing. And while you're in the RUT, you begin to lose hope and faith. You bury your superpowers, and you nestle in with all the other powerless people who are in that RUT with you. (This is why the friends and the company you keep are so important, but we'll talk about that in another chapter). But what you're missing is that no one and nothing can strip you of your power - it's yours. And even though you took a tough blow, and thought you lost power – you did not. The lights went out, but there is still power. The passion for your purpose and the vision you have for your life is your power. So long as there is a part of you that craves and desires a better and more fulfilled life, there is always power. And no one can take that away from you. Up to now, you may have transferred your power from your purpose to your feelings of inadequacy or frustration, but the power to change and get out of your RUT still belongs to you. Redirect your energy from feeling sorry for yourself to being empowered to change and live your best life starting today. Decide to get out of your RUT! Reclaim your power. Reconnect it to your passion and the life you crave and declare yourself powerful. Get ignited, get empowered, and be the incredible person you were meant to be.

I'm no stranger to being in a RUT. I've been in a RUT one, two, three, okay... I stopped counting after awhile. Let's just say, I've been a RUT more times than I'd like to admit. I'm human. I've made mistakes, been irresponsible and walked out of purpose many times in my life. And that's okay. The goal is not to never fall or make mistakes. The goal is to stand up when you fall, learn from your mistakes, come back stronger, better, and wiser. The goals are the lessons learned, the testimony from the test, and turning mind-grenades and misery into victory and vision that become reality.

In 1995, (my junior year in college), as I sat across from the Dean of Student of my college, I listened sadly, and totally embarrassed, as she told my parents that I was being suspended for one semester because of bad grades and inappropriate campus conduct. Listening to her and watching the disappointment on my parents' faces was one of the most horrifying experiences I have ever gone through to date. My parents did not send me to college for me to come home, suspended, without a college degree. I found myself in an awful time and place in my life. I disappointed my parents, wasted their money and made a mockery of my life. I screwed up big time. I was ashamed, humiliated, and sorry for letting down the people that worked so hard to help me be successful. I felt so bad because not only did I let my foolishness get way out of control, but I knew better and should have never gotten into that type of trouble in the first place. I didn't grow up a misfit! I was a gifted student. I went to church every Sunday. I was a talented singer, artist, storyteller, and writer. I knew the importance of education and the value of time and money, yet I went to college and temporarily lost my mind – to say the least. And while I was losing my mind, I was losing sight of who I was and everything that made me brilliant, beautiful, and unique. I was in a RUT. That suspension forced me to take a long look at my life - specifically my choices and where I was exerting all my energy. I realized that I needed to reconnect to the core of who I was. I was an ambitious introvert that craved success. I wasn't a trouble-maker, drop out, or a quitter. I had to get back to Me! I'd lost myself trying to be someone that I wasn't; trying to fit in and be liked. And it wasn't working; I wasn't fitting in and while people may or may not have like me, I damn sure didn't like myself. I needed to change and redirect my energy. My parents encouraged me to go back to the same college that suspended me, but I made the decision to stay away from that college and enroll into a college closer to home. I concluded that the school away from home was not the right place for "Me". I had an opportunity for a second chance and a new direction: I could get up and try again. And this time, I was focused on my education and my goal was my degree. I walked in my truth and pursued my purpose with passion. I was not worried about being liked. I worried about my grades and focused on my vision, the bigger picture of my life. This time around, I was smarter and better prepared and equipped for the journey. I also knew that I did not want to make the same mistakes again so I made conscious efforts to make better choices, improved how I sought out relationships, and was very intentional about my success in school. It was during this pivotal time in my life where I experienced firsthand what happens when you get disconnect from your goals and start to take wrong action in your life. And I also experienced and reaped the benefits of getting out of my RUT, learning from my mistakes and mind-grenades, and pushing forward – revived, renewed, and committed to my vision. I'd lost control of my life and the events that had taken place were all a byproduct of being lost, walking out of purpose, and out of control. And the reason I lost control was because I became detached from my commitment and passion for my purpose. I decided to rise up from my RUT, ignite my inner fuse, and on September 9, 1999, I stood on the stage of Temple University and received my Bachelor Degree in Finance while my parents stood proudly cheering me on as I walked across the graduation stage. When I look back on that whole terrible mess, I see now that it was the best thing that happened to me. You see, I needed to get knocked down in order to rise up brighter, better, smarter, and more prepared than ever to be the person that I was divinely called to be. It was through that storm that "A Life Ignited" was born.

It's important to remember this: That "thing" you just came out of, or you're going through now, does not define you. It does not tell your entire story. Regardless of where you've been and what you've been through, it's time for you to get up, dust off the guilt and shame, and go after your dreams and all that you desire. But remember, desire isn't enough! Desire without action is only a wish. And action without preparation and focus is a like a journey without a destination. You may find yourself making moves and taking some steps, but without direction and clear focus about where you are going, what you are doing, and why you are doing it, you'll always find yourself in the same state: a state of desire where you never accomplish anything. You'll remain on the path to nowhere. Until you plan and prepare yourself for success, you will never quite achieve it.

The good news is that this book will help you plan, focus, and ask the tough questions you need to ask yourself in order to move confidently in the direction of your dreams. This will be your handbook for igniting the fuse inside so you can start living your life ignited.

The most powerful weapon on earth is the human
soul on fire.
- Ferdinand Foch

A life ignited. I've used the term several times now, and I titled this book *A Life Ignited.* I created the phrase and made it the staple term of my business and my personal life because it truly embodies all that I am. A life ignited is "a life of purpose, on purpose, and in motion." Let's dissect the meaning of this powerful term.

A life of purpose is one that is vision driven. When you live a life "of purpose", everything you do is based on where you desire to be. You make decisions that are going to get you closer to realizing your dreams and making your vision a reality. When you are vision driven and you're living a life of purpose, your dreams are non-negotiable. You are unapologetic to the decisions you make and the things that you do because you understand that you have a destination you are trying to reach, and in order get there, certain things need to be done and other things (and people) need to be given lower priority or cut out from your life altogether. When I was living out of purpose, I was negotiating my dreams so people would like me or approve of my decisions. I was playing Russian roulette with my dreams. I wasn't living of purpose; I wasn't guided by my passion to get out of the neighborhood I grew up in and have a better life than the one that I saw many people around me live. When you live a life of purpose, you have laser focus on your goals. You know exactly what you are striving for and you don't let anyone or anything get in your way.

A life on purpose is a life lived intentionally. Every day your vision and your goals are top of mind. You make good choices and your actions are parallel to the vision you have for your life. You work hard not to disrespect yourself or your purpose. You intentionally eat healthy foods, you make time to read books, and you purposefully network and seek out people who are like-minded and driven just like you. You're strategic about the choices you make and the things you do because you understand that the actions you take will either make or break your ability to fulfill your goals. There is too much at risk not to be intentional with your decisions and choices. You know where you are going, and you work purposefully to make good things happen in your life.

A life in motion means you have things to do and places to go. You are driven to get results. There is no time to sit around, wishing and hoping for things to happen to you. You don't cross your fingers and hope your dreams will fall into your lap. You stir up the universe around you as you excel and soar towards your purpose with passion. You work diligently and confidently. You take the right actions, and you reap the benefits of your diligence, resilience, and hard work. You are motivated and on the move.

To sum it up, when you live a life ignited, you have desire, you take action, and you see results.

- When you live a life of purpose, you have a desire outcome
  You have goals you want to accomplish and a vision for your life

- When you live a life on purpose, you are intentional
  You focus on achieving your goals

- When you live a life in motion, you take right actions

You do the work and get results. You accomplish your goals

What sets apart someone who is "a life ignited" from someone who is lying dormant like an unignited firework in a box somewhere? The person who embodies the spirit of "a life ignited" understands that they need to move with purpose at all times despite the obstacles that come their way. They are committed to the vision they have for their life. They will not let anything stop them. A person who lives a life ignited understands that yes, you will get knocked off track: Life happens. There will be plot twists in your story and they will come when you least expect it. But people who live a life ignited keep moving and pushing anyway. They don't give up when life hits them hard. They don't stop at the first sign of adversity. And they may find themselves in a RUT, but they don't stay there. On the other hand, people who don't live a life ignited do three things consistently: They blame other people for their problems, they make excuses, and stay in their RUT's. If you are just going through the motions and living as a victim of circumstance, you are not living your life ignited. If you are comfy cozy in your RUT, then you are definitely not living a life ignited. If you are not living a purpose-driven life, you are not living a life ignited. If you are not living a life ignited, you are living below your God-given appointed position of greatness, and it's time to stand up, step out, and achieve all the things you desire for yourself and those you love. Life has so much to offer you, and wasting another day wishing, hoping, and deferring your dreams makes a travesty of the gift of wonderful life God has given you. And despite what it looks or feels like, you are blessed, your life is important and necessary, and you have the potential to live your life ignited right now.

Like I told you earlier, I wasn't always living a life ignited. I found myself getting really messy and one day, when I looked up and looked around, I was completely disconnected from my purpose. I learned from my mistakes and became a better person because of the struggles I faced and overcame. I walked with crazy faith, and didn't let fear and obstacles keep me from walking in my purpose. When you live a life ignited, you are not exempt from the struggles and pains of life. But when you live a life ignited, you are determined and strong. You scratch and claw your way through the battles and the hardships, knowing you must get through the rain to see your rainbow. You understand that stars shine brightest in darkness and know that disappointments are as natural to life as a sunrise, a sunset, the moon, and the stars. But, you never give up. Instead, you get up, you keep moving, and you fight for the life you know you deserve to live. You understand that the more you try to rise above mediocrity, failure, guilt and shame more obstacles and tests will be thrown at you. You'll constantly be tested, but when you are "A Life Ignited", you are empowered by the unwavering and uncompromising vision for your life.

I wrote *A life Ignited* to help people who are stuck in a RUT, not living in their purpose, and not working at their fullest potential start to live ignited lives by inspiring and motivating them to believe in the power they possess to make positive changes in their lives. You are greater and better than you can imagine. Your divine calling is not in that RUT. It's outside of your comfort zone; waiting for you to show up, get ignited, and bless the world with your gifts and talents. A life ignited is about creating a meaningful life and living your life to the fullest: a life of purpose, on purpose, and in motion: A life that you are proud of. In this book, I wrote from my heart just for you, I will help you get recharged for your journey and motivate you along the way.

I'm ready for you to reach your goals, walk in purpose, and experience the abundance, prosperity, and happiness you crave.

Are you ready to be unstoppable and explosive?

Get ready to "Get Ignited!"

GET UP

Our greatest glory is not in never falling
but in rising every time we fall.
—Confucius

AS I THINK ABOUT MY college suspension, I realize that season of suffering was one of the best things that ever happened to me. You see, my breakthrough was in the rebuilding process. But in order to be rebuilt stronger and better, I had to first, get up.

Living a life ignited is not about having the "perfect life". Living a life ignited is accepting that as you journey towards the success, fulfillment, and life you crave, you will be met with obstacles and disappointments along the way. You know this. You anticipate this. You prepare for them. And when they appear, you attack them. You crush them. Now, let's be real: There will be times when you look and feel like you lost the battle. But when you live a life ignited, you don't surrender your goals and dreams to the enemy you're facing, because what appears to be pay cuts and setbacks will turn out to be pay increases and setups for comebacks. I know all about fighting battles and thinking I lost them to find out later, as I continued to persevere—worn, battered, and bruised—that I actually won the whole war. When you triumph over tests, those tests become your testimonies. You continue to fight because every testimony moves you one step closer to living your life ignited.

> *There's no passion to be found playing small - in settling for a life that is less than you are capable of living.*
> *- Nelson Mandela*

Remember Dorothy's journey to The Emerald City in The Wizard of Oz? Do you remember all the roadblocks and challenges Dorothy faced as she tried to get back home? I love Dorothy's story because it's a metaphor for endurance and resilience despite the booby traps and difficulties we have to confront when we strive to live our lives ignited. Dorothy was brave. She fought here way, in ruby red slippers and all, to the Emerald City. And once she was there, even after finding out that the wizard had no power to get her home, she didn't give up. She tapped into the greatness within, that was with her all along, clicked her heels, and found her way back to where she belonged - home. She never second-guessed her vision. Dorothy proceeded with passion because she was driven with purpose. Her goal was to get home. And despite the difficulty of the journey, she did.

Right now, you may be having a Dorothy moment in your life. You're lost and you are desperately trying to find your way back to happiness, peace, fulfillment, health – and maybe even love. You're wondering, *"How the heck can I get out of this mess? Where do I even start?"* There is something in you that knows you are not tapping into your greatness in a certain area of your life. You want to be a better version of yourself. The person you are today is awesome and people may even praise and adore you because you have so many great qualities, but deep within, you know there is a part of you that does not operate at its fullest potential. And that part of you is a vital organ in the body of your brilliance. You are reading this book because you are ready to give life to the most inner parts of yourself that are unhappy, unfulfilled, and sad about the RUT you've found yourself in. You know you deserve better and should be proud of yourself in this moment for taking steps to revive and reconnect the most amazing version of yourself to the vision you have for your life. You may not know it, so I'm going to let you in on a little secret – your ambition, your curiosity, and your initiative to find answers are all superpowers you possess. And while you may not recognize it, I'm letting you know now that you are tapping into your greatest potential simply by taking the steps to read this book, learn, and grow.

I want you to take a moment or two and answer these questions. They will remind you why it's important for you to get up out of your RUT. Remember, your breakthrough is in the "get up".

Give yourself time to think about each question. Answer honestly.

- What is your Emerald City?
  What is your goal or desire?

- Why do want to reach your Emerald City?
  Why is it so important that you reach your goals/vision?

- Who is the wicked witch in your life trying to keep you away from your Emerald City?
  This can be a person, place, or things. What is stopping you or trying to stop you?

- How have you given your wicked witch permission and power to keep you down or hold you back?
  Self-reflect on how you handle obstacles and adversity

- Were you able to successfully defeat the wicked witch in the past? How or why not?
  How did you engage or disengage your greatness and super powers in the past?

- If you feel as though you are knocked down right now, how can you draw from your past successes or failures to defeat the wicked witch now?
  How can your lessons learned from past experiences help you today?

- What's at stake if you don't make it to The Emerald City?

What's the alternative to reaching your goals? What does that image look like?

Dorothy defeated her wicked witch and you will defeat yours, too. But, the first thing you must do is get up! When you get knocked down, get up! There is no power in lying down. There is no victory in defeat. Right now, in this very moment, as you read this book, you may feel as though you are down. Time and time again, you've tried to get better and do better, but you feel defeated because you keep falling down and you don't see or feel that you are making progress. You may be tired and frustrated, but you are not defeated. Get up!

> *Weeping may endure for a night, but joy cometh in*
> *the morning.*
> *Psalms 30:5*

Your goal is not going to come to you. You've got to press your way toward it. Your life ignited is waiting for you to claim it. You may be under construction, but the road to your goals and dreams is not closed. Get up and continue your journey. Go get what is yours: your life ignited!

> *The only person who can pull me down is myself,*
> *and I'm not going to let myself pull me down anymore. -*
> *C. JoyBell C.*

When you get up and stand, you are able to fight for your right to live in abundance and prosperity. If you've ever seen a boxing match, you know that once your opponent knocks you down, you're powerless. The fight is at a standstill until you get

5

up. You have to get up to keep going. You cannot fight when you are down. You've got to muster all the strength inside you and lift yourself up, inch by inch and muscle by muscle. Get up and stand because you know you deserve better. Get up and stand because you are strong and resilient. Get up and stand because you've fought too hard for too long to give up now. Get up and stand because if you don't, you'll have to settle for what you have now: a life below your fullest potential that doesn't make you happy. You deserve so much more than that.

Many people are not living ignited lives, and have instead settled for mediocrity because they do not get up and stand after they get knocked down. Don't allow that to be your story. Do not be defeated by setbacks, moments of weakness, or feelings of frustration. Okay, so you got knocked down or your strategy didn't go the way you thought it was going to go. That happens. Actually, it happens to everyone who's ever tried to reach a goal. If success were easy, everyone would be successful all the time at everything they tried to accomplish.

The journey to success comes with quite a few failures along the way, but in my experience, failure precedes success. When you are trying to do something incredible, you will fail along the way. Sometimes, you will mess up. You will get in your own way. You will make bad choices, but remember that failure is not a reason to stop, drop, and give up. Failure is actually a checkpoint. If you fail, take a moment to observe what happened, understand what went wrong—why it went wrong—and determine what you can do better or differently as you continue to move forward. Failure is an opportunity to learn from your mistakes. Failure is where you reinvent your process, realign and refocus on your target, reconnect your passion to your purpose, and reappear stronger and better. Each failure will bring you one step closer to reaching your goals. Failure is an opportunity to start again.

The first thing I want you to do right now is get up. If you are sitting down, stand up. Yes stand up on your two feet right now, wherever you are. If you physically can't stand, pump your fist in the air. So what if someone looks at you like you are weird or crazy? They don't know your struggle or your story. So who cares? Just get up right now as a personal declaration to yourself that you are not knocked down or out. You are still on your journey to living the life you envision for yourself. You may have to dust yourself off—and you may be a little wounded and bruised because of what life threw at you—but you're ready to stand stronger and better than ever. Be open to learning from your experiences and taking steps to change your mind-set and behaviors for the purpose of being positioned for progress and prosperity.

Today is a new day with a new opportunity to work towards your goals and dreams. Get up!
- Rhonda Kinard

Very early in life, I learned the importance of getting up and standing in the face of fear and adversity. I can remember my first, and only, fistfight. I was in the fifth grade. This one girl would terrorize all the other girls in the schoolyard at recess. She would take their snacks, pull their hair, knock them down, and on occasion punch a girl in the face for no reason. This was back in the eighties, way before all the anti-bullying campaigns and such we have now. And even though there were adults around, she was not deterred from kicking, punching, and fighting. She had free reign over the schoolyard. She was the oppressive dictator of Hamilton Elementary School schoolyard. Her name was Vicki. She had a posse of mini Vicki's that she bred, or maybe frightened, into little bullies, too.

When the other girls and I saw this little posse of Vicki's coming our way, we would all get anxious because we knew they were nothing but trouble. The Vicki's went looking for trouble, and if they couldn't find any, they would create some. On this one particular day, my friends and I were jumping rope, laughing, and having fun during recess. The posse of Vicki's came over, and dictator Vicki snatched the rope from one of my friends. When she snatched the rope, it flew through the air and it hit my cheek before it fell to the ground. It stung as it snapped across my face, and it left a big, red welt on my cheek. I was—and in many ways, I still am—an introvert. As a kid, I was a tiny, skinny little thing. I was very quiet, and I didn't like trouble of any kind. I got along well with everybody. And up to this point, I'd had no problems with Vicki. She'd never bothered my friends or me before this point. We were always watching for her and her posse, because we knew they were trouble, but somehow we stayed under her radar – until now. I'd seen her antagonize other girls and boys and always felt bad for the kids she bullied. But on this day, it was my turn to face the fear of the schoolyard – Vicki. I grabbed my face where the rope hit me, looked up at Vicki (who was at least a foot taller than I was), and said, "The rope just hit my face!"

She said, "So what?" Her facial expression made it clear that she did not care.

I walked up to her and tried to snatch the rope from her, but she moved her arm quickly so I could not reach it. I looked up at her again and said in as stern a voice as possible, "You're going to give us our rope back, and you're going to go away!"

By that time, a crowd had formed around us. Everyone in the schoolyard was watching. No one was saying a word. There was dead silence. With my heart pounding, I waited for Vicki's response to my demands.

She took a few steps closer to me, and without warning, she pushed me to the ground. I fell flat on my butt. I was so scared. I thought, *Rhonda, why did you ever say anything to this crazy girl? She is definitely going to kill you now.* Then I thought, *Well, if I am going to die today, I'm not going to die lying down on the dirty ground.* So I got up. But when I got up, to my surprise, I didn't feel like a victim. I felt like a warrior – I felt powerful and bigger than myself. I knew it was now or never. I had to let Vicki know she would not intimidate me anymore.

I charged Vicki. I ran toward big Vicki with my head down and arms and fists wailing. Now, do you know the story of David and Goliath? Remember how little David defeated big Goliath? Well, this story does not end that way. As I charged Vicki, my face met her fist. She punched me right in the nose. I remember a sharp pain running through my nose straight up to my forehead. I grabbed my face and when I looked down at my hand, there was lots of blood on my fingers. Before I could react, a lunchtime aid broke up the fight and instructed the crowd of students to disperse. Much of what happened in the next moments is a blur, but I do remember ending up in the principal's office. I sat there and waited for my nose to stop bleeding. I think the school nurse checked me out to make sure my nose wasn't broken, but I can't remember. As I walked back to my classroom, I was embarrassed that I was beaten up in front of everyone and ashamed that I had been in a fistfight. When I got back to my classroom, to my surprise, no one made fun of me. Actually, everyone gave me sympathetic smiles—the kind you give people when you feel bad for them and want to show your support at the same time. I was still pretty worried that the Vicki's would come for me after school, but they didn't. They never bothered my friends or me again. That was the first and last time anyone ever bullied me.

That experience taught me that you have to go to battle with your obstacles and meet them head on. If I hadn't fought her, I would have been scared and fearful every day after that. Yes, she knocked me down and gave me a bloody nose, but in the end, I won. I began to enjoy recess and the Vicki's were not a threat to my jump rope buddies and me ever again.

Like Vicki, obstacles can appear very scary. Many of them seem overwhelming. But a strong sense of purpose and faith in your talents and gifts will stomp out and defeat obstacles and naysayers any day. Here are a few examples of famous people you may have heard of that had to overcome incredible obstacles. Just imagine, as you read about each person, if they did not get up when they got knocked down.

Oprah Winfrey

Her setbacks included being fired from her job as a television reporter because she was not a good fit for television.

Theodor Seuss Geisel (Dr. Seuss)

Twenty-seven different publishers rejected Dr. Seuss's first book *To Think That I Saw It on Mulberry Street.*

Michael Jordan

He was cut from his high school basketball team because he wasn't a good player.

Barbara Corcoran

Her boyfriend walked out the door after being caught cheating with his secretary. He told Barbara, "You'll never succeed without me." She ended up being a millionaire, a real estate mogul, and an entrepreneur.

Steven Spielberg

This household name dropped out of high school and applied to film school three times, but he was unsuccessful due to his grades.

Walt Disney
The editor of a newspaper fired him for lacking ideas.

John Paul DeJoria

He went from being homeless to becoming CEO of John Paul Mitchell Systems (hair care company) and a billionaire.

Imagine how our lives would be impacted if these people did not crush mind-grenades, getup, dust themselves off, and chase their dreams? They remind us that success came after they got up – which means they had setbacks and situations occur that knocked them down, too.

> *It's not whether you get knocked down, it's whether*
> *you get up.*
> *- Vince Lombardi*

> *The breakthrough is in the "Get Up"!*
> *- Rhonda Kinard*

Now they are living ignited lives. They didn't let obstacles, opinions, disappointment, and even rejection stand in the way of the vision they had for their lives! And there is no reason why you cannot have the same tenacity and resilience to follow your dreams and realize your vision. Remember, before they were famous, they were simply ordinary people who believed in themselves and their dreams, and then decided to do extraordinary things. They got up, pressed on, and now they are living ignited lives - and blessing the world with their talents and gifts.

I've been knocked down pretty hard on many occasions. I've been hurt. I've been talked about and judged. I've been taken advantage of and taken for granted. I've also made dumb mistakes, acted like an idiot, and I've been disobedient. My journey spared me no expense for my immaturity, foolish behaviors, and failures. These experiences did not break me though –they actually made me tougher. When I fused all my good and bad experiences together, the result was a stronger, focused woman who was determined to rise out of her RUT and go after her dreams. I learned from my mistakes and pushed forward, becoming better than I was the day before. And today, because of my experiences, what I learned from them, and what they made of me, I am "A Life Ignited".

It doesn't matter what you've gone through or what you are going through right now, get up, dust yourself off, and know this is only a bump in the road. Your journey is not over. Actually, it has just begun. You have the ability—no matter where you are right now—to get up. It's time to continue your journey to living your life ignited. Get up and fight for your goals and dreams. Get up so you can go after the life you desire, deserve and crave.

CHANGE

If you do what you've always done, you'll get what
you've always gotten.
-Henry Ford

FIREWORKS IN THEIR IGNITED STATE are magical, but prior to being ignited, fireworks are pretty boring. Once the fuse of a firework is ignited, heat is produced and explosive energy is released. The firework soars into the sky and transforms from a state of lifelessness to being radiant, unstoppable, and explosive. Have you ever seen someone light a firework? They'll light the fuse and run for cover because once that fuse is lit, that firework cannot be contained. If you get in its way, you might get hurt because nothing is going to keep that firework down.

Strength does not come from physical capacity. It
comes from indomitable will.
- Mahatma Gandhi

Just as fireworks transform the moment their fuses are lit, you too can ignite your inner fuse, transform your life, and become just as uncompromising and powerful as a firework erupting in the sky. If you want to soar, transform, be luminous and light up the night sky in your life, you have to change and evolve. And just like a firework that has been ignited, you must fully commit to changing yourself. Your transformation to living your life ignited begins with getting up out of your RUT and committing to change.

Change is the idea of transforming into something better than you were: A more productive, powerful, and passionate version of yourself. Change means doing something different or acting differently. Change is required if you want to reach your goals.

Admitting that change is necessary is the first and most important step in any personal growth journey. Most people are not self-aware enough to know that change is required in them. They blame everyone and everything else for their problems or failures. They never challenge themselves to make changes in their lives that will improve the outcomes of the situations they find themselves in. And since we do not have control over everyone and everything else, we must be committed to changing our actions, thoughts, and behaviors. If you want to change your circumstance and elevate your life and your mind-set, you must be ready and willing to change yourself.

Those who cannot change their minds cannot change
anything.
-George Bernard Shaw

There was a period of time when my husband was driving me nuts in our marriage. I would talk to my mom every morning on my way to work about how uncooperative or irrational he was being about certain things. One particular day, I was yet again dumping on my mom about my husband and how he did this and said that and how he needed to fix this and that. As I was ranting on, my mom interrupted me and said, "Wow! You sure are negative." *What? Me?* I was completely taken aback. I was stunned because first off, she was supposed to be on my side agreeing with everything I said, and secondly, I'm the least negative person I know. (See how we don't always admit that "we" need to change?)

I said, "No, I'm not negative. He's wrong and I'm simply pointing out what he needs to resolve within himself so we can move forward in our marriage."

In a very unconvincing tone, my mom said, "Okay." My mom gave me the dignity of allowing me to defend myself some more, but I could tell from her silence as we moved along in the conversation that she was not buying my argument. After we hung up, I thought about what she said. *Am I really being negative? Could I be part of the problem?* I thought about her words. I took a very uncomfortable look at my behavior and realized that she was right. I needed to change. I needed to change how I spoke to my husband, how I approached him, and how I asked him to do things. I realized that while my husband may have done things I didn't find favor with, my aggression, my attitude, and my mind-set were making matters worse. I was contributing to the discontent in our home with my approach to resolution. My husband is my best friend and a big piece of my world: I needed to find a different way to resolve conflict with him. And I did just that. I changed how I spoke to him. I change my negative attitude and my tone of voice. Within days after I made a few minor adjustments, there was a major shift in our relationship. Our communication got better almost instantly. And because he could actually hear me, he was able to understand me, and we were able to fix the things that were broken – together.

> *Your problem isn't the problem. Your reaction is the problem.*
> *-Anonymous*

Changing one's self is one of the most difficult things a person has to do. So many people live below their potential because they have to change in order to rise above their current situations. And since, most times, change comes in the form of hard work, most people decide—consciously or subconsciously— not to do the hard work required to live at the incredible and ignited levels they are capable of.

> *When obstacles arise, you change your direction to reach your goal—you do not change your decision to get there.*
> *- Zig Ziglar*

If you want firework status in your life, you have to change. And in order to change, you need to know the recipe for sustainable change in your life. For clarity's sake, I've broken down the idea of change into four parts. Each of the components listed below is an essential element of change. I call them "The Four C's of Change".

The Four C's of Change

- commitment
- creativity
- challenge
- consistency

Commitment to Change

If you want more, you must change. If you want to improve, you must change. If you want growth, you must change. No matter what you want to upgrade or enhance, committing to change is the first step to improving it. If you are not committed, you'll find yourself right back in the same place next year or even next month trying to figure out why you've had no progress and why you are no closer to reaching your goals.

Commitment is a sense of being obligated to something. When you are committed to something, you make sacrifices for its success and you do not give up on it because it looks hard or the journey becomes challenging. When you are fully committed, you are totally engaged. When you are committed to something, you not only show up, but you show out –excelling and exceeding your own expectations. Commitment is a promise of devotion and endless effort to making sure you always do and give your best.

Before we move any further, I want to make sure that we are on the same page about being 'committed'. I want to define 'committed' for you - a life ignited style. Sometimes people mistake being committed with 'going through the motions'. Let's make sure you can distinguish between the two. Just because we are following certain processes, moving in certain directions, and saying certain things, does not mean that we are committed to something [or someone]. For many of us, we are just going through the motions. Being committed and going through the motions of change look very similar, but there is one major component that sets them completely apart. When you are committed, you are *dedicated* to the vision you have for your life. And that dedication is the glue that bonds your commitment to your goals and dreams. When we are going through the motions, we show up and we do a little hard work, but when the obstacles arise, we give up and decide that we don't want to do the hard work anymore. We quit when it's no longer easy or fun. But when you are committed to something, you are dedicated to the bigger and better purpose of your life. The commitment goes far beyond the immediate goal. I may not want to go to the gym or workout some nights, but I push myself. Not because of the goal to get to the gym 4 – 5 times a week, but because my heart health depends on my showing up and being dedicated to my vision of being hypertension and medication free. I cannot give up on my health because if I do I may die of a heart attack or a stroke. I can't just go through the motions because not taking care of myself is not an option for me. Being committed is not just about doing the feel good work and dancing with unicorns under rainbows. It's about working, fighting, and moving towards your vision – without compromise and without option to quit.

I think of times in my life when I thought I was committed to something, but later realized after my lack of commitment revealed its self, that even though I was participating and going through the motions, I wasn't fully engaged or making the necessary sacrifices required in order to be successful. As a freshman entering college, I wasn't really committed to my education or my college experience. Yes, I traveled from my hometown of Philly to Hampton, Virginia, to attend college. Yes, I took out student loans for the majority of my tuition and room and board expenses. Yes, I attended classes and even went to the library from time to time and joined study groups, but despite all this 'preparation' and 'action', I wasn't really committed. When I arrived on campus, I spent more time worrying about looking cute, making friends, being liked, and nurturing an unhealthy romance than I did on my education. I knew I wanted to go to college so I could have a good life with a better lifestyle than the one I was raised in. I wanted these things and much more, but I wasn't putting in the work required to achieve them. This lack of commitment, along with my mounting bad decisions and bad grades (okay, terrible grades—mostly Fs) caught up with me. Eventually, I was suspended from college for one semester. And as I mentioned before, the suspension was a by-product of being totally unfocused and uncommitted to what was really important to me. I knew I needed to reconnect my passion to my purpose and recommit to what was important in my life. At the time, that was my education. Being suspended from college was a real wakeup call that forced me to realize I was not committed to changing my future. If I didn't want to end up being mediocre, poor, and frustrated, I needed to commit to change. And I did just that! I rededicated myself to my studies, my education, and my future. I committed to being a serious student, and more importantly, I committed to being a better person. I got up, changed my direction, and became fully engaged in my education and future, and I did not compromise the two ever again.

As I contemplated change, I considered my poor choices and the stupid and silly things that led to my suspension and overall unproductive college experience. Not studying was a choice. Sleeping late and being lazy was a choice. Skipping class to be with my boyfriend was a choice. These poor choices and lack of commitment to my goals cost me greatly. I took an honest look at what I screwed up and then committed to not making those mistakes again. And I didn't make them again. I learned from my mistakes and I made decisions that supported my purpose. First, I decided that being away from home while I went to college was toxic for me. I wasn't ready for that type of responsibility, and even though my parents supported me and encouraged me to go back to Virginia the following semester, I decided not to go back to school away from home. Instead, I enrolled in a local university where I finished my undergraduate degree program. I eventually graduated with an excellent grade point average and a great job.

When you decide to change, you are committing to a lifestyle change. If you are not committing to a lifestyle change for the long haul, you will not be able to sustain the results of change. It's no different than someone going on a fad diet and losing lots of weight in a fairly short period of time. They may lose the weight quickly, but because they were not committed to transformation and the process of change, they are unable to sustain the weight loss. When you see them again a year later, the weight's back on. Quick fixes are meant to be temporary solutions. And temporary solutions will not help you sustain a life ignited. Who wants to do well, smell the scent of success, and go backward again? The goal is to ignite the fuse that lives within and be able to sustain that fire and energy for a lifetime. Commitment to change is the precursor to achieving and sustaining ignited status in your life.

So, as you sit and think about your life and how, just like I, you may have screwed up opportunities, ruined relationships, packed on the pounds, or blocked a blessing, I want you to remember that you can [re]commit to change right now and begin to repair that which has been broken. Decide today to be fully engaged in your success and pursue your goals as if your life depends on it – in some cases, it does. Commit to being better than ever and rising out of your RUT. Commit to igniting your inner fuse by changing how you've done things in the past. Commit to planning and preparing for prosperity in your life. Commit to success and reaching your goals by committing to and being open to changing that which does not work in your favor as you pursue your goals and your life ignited.

Creativity in Change

In John Maxwell's bestselling book, *How Successful People Think,* he refers to creativity as an "unhampered view of reality". Creativity is when your mind can conceive different ways of doing things, handling situations, and reaching your goals beyond what you see every day and what others around you have accepted as the one and only "right" way. Uncreative people make excuses. Creative people find a way or make a new way. When you live a life ignited you are creative. You make a way, you find the way, you invent the way but you don't give up because the way you were used to taking did not lead to the success and fulfillment you desire.

> *There is no doubt that creativity is the most*
> *important human resource of all. Without creativity,*
> *there would be no progress, and we would be forever*
> *repeating the same patterns.*
> - Edward de Bono

Change requires us to utilize creativity as a way to shift our thinking and break the monotonous habits that no longer serve us. Creativity is all about coming up with new ideas and insights in order to move ahead. Open-mindedness, flexibility, and willingness to pursue different opportunities are critical components in the transformation process. Creativity allows you to start thinking outside of the mediocrity box.

As a licensed Realtor in Pennsylvania, I welcomed the technological advancements that positively impacted our industry in the early 2000's. New software applications, websites, and phone apps changed the way Realtors were able to connect and conduct business with clients and other cooperating real estate agents. These new tools allowed me to be more effective and efficient in my business. During this time, my clients were mostly real estate investors, and because of these advances in technology, I didn't have to drag them to a real estate office or a title company for settlements. We were able to conduct closings at Starbucks and sometimes at their places of business –thanks to an Internet connection and savvy, web-based software and tools. These new tools allowed Realtors to be creative in our approach to our business and how we worked with each client to meet their unique needs. Even though many of these new technologies undoubtedly introduced better approaches to many of the prehistoric processes that were being used, many of the non-creative and less open-minded Realtors I worked with did not want to use these new technologies. In some brokerages, policies forced Realtors to maintain the old way of doing things. In the instances where I worked with people who were not open to creative change, transactions were a real challenge. As the world changed, the needs and communication expectations of the customers we were serving changed too. We needed to be as flexible as the world we lived in. I changed the way I did business to meet the needs and demands of my changing "client-scape". Creatively serving my clients ensured that they kept coming back to me when it was time to buy or sell a house. I worked with the same investors (and non-investor buyers and sellers) in multiple transactions over several years because of my honest, efficient and creative approach to my real estate business.

Not only did my real estate business require creativity in change, but so did my health and wellness journey. I became very creative with how I would ensure I was eating nutritious foods every day. I didn't always have time to prepare a complete nutritious meal with fresh veggies and all the essential nutrients recommended by my physician. But instead of making excuses for why I was not getting my vitamins and nutrients, I found a creative way to get the nutrition my body needed. I started drinking fruit and vegetable smoothies. They were quick and easy to make and provided all the nutrients and vitamins recommended by my doctor in just one delicious drink. Now I'll be honest with you – a handful of spinach, a banana, rice milk, pineapple juice and chia seeds blended together with ice sounded totally disgusting to me at first. But eventually, I looked beyond the ingredients and focused on the benefits. To my surprise, blended together, they were delicious. Who knew a drink made of spinach and fruit could taste so darn good? My creative approach to my dietary needs helped reduce my high blood pressure, maintain my healthy living goals, and helped me improve my overall quality of life.

Creativity in change is also an ongoing necessity in my marriage. I've been married almost fifteen years, and what I know through experience is that marriage is a feat of faith that requires creativity as you learn to effectively communicate, coexist, fulfill, and support one another through the different phases of your marriage and your life as a person. Creativity is at the core of two people being fulfilled and happy in a marriage over a lifetime. Marriages become boring and frustrating when both spouses are not equally committed to breaking up the monotony, trying new things, and exploring new options. Creativity in change has allowed me to support my husband and love him through the various stages of our lives—through the ups and downs and the good and the not so great times. Creativity has allowed me to be a better wife and friend to him. Creativity in change makes it possible for romance and passion to be alive and very well after almost twenty years of togetherness and intimacy.

Creativity in change is required so you can continue or start to improve any relationship or situation you are in. Creativity in change is the key to breaking the chains of monotony and bad habits. Be open to creativity. Welcome new insights and new ideas. When someone suggests a new idea, don't be so quick to brush it off or cast it down. Allow yourself the freedom to experience new opportunities and new mind-sets. Be a creative thinker – open to new or unfamiliar ideas. After all, the old way you've been doing things hasn't always worked out for you, has it? Be creative in your journey. Discover and explore new strategies. Be open-minded and allow for new doors to open. Be creative as you change.

The Challenge of Change

If change were easy, imagine how many things all of us would have accomplished in our lives. But the reality is change is not easy, and it can be quite a challenge. Change is one of the most difficult things in life for us to accept. But even though change can be difficult, it is not impossible. And the more you focus on the vision you have for your life, the more welcoming you will be to the challenges of change.

> *The brick walls are there for a reason. The brick walls*
> *are not there to keep us out. The brick walls are there to*
> *give us a chance to show how badly we want something.*
> *Because the brick walls are there to stop the people who*

don't want it badly enough. They're there to stop the
other people.

-Randy Pausch

What is a challenge? A challenge is an invitation to endure obstacles during a season of discomfort in order to get to a better place of success or satisfaction. A challenge completed symbolizes character, personal growth, resilience, and inner strength.

If you pay close attention to the definition of a challenge, you will see that a challenge is a great thing. Challenges can be wonderfully fulfilling—if you stick them out until the end and don't quit during the season of discomfort. As you journey towards your life ignited, you will encounter problems. There will be trials and trouble along the way. But understand that you are in a challenge and in order to get to your appointed position of prosperity, you must first get through the season of discomfort. Do not see your obstacles as isolated problems. Understand that they are part of the challenge and were put in your path as part of the growth and change process. Those obstacles in your way are there to make you stronger and to prepare you for prosperity. At the end of the season of discomfort, there is success and fulfillment, but you have to accept the challenge, stick with it, beat all odd and obstacles, and see it to completion.

Being challenged in life is inevitable, being defeated is
optional.

-Roger Crawford

Coming back home to Philadelphia to pursue the remainder of my undergraduate studies at Temple University was one of the most challenging times of my life. When I started going to Temple, I had lots of catching up to do academically. I had wasted so much time goofing off in Virginia that I had barely learned anything, and I had to make up all the classes I had failed. Getting back on track was quite the challenge. I cried many nights—and days too. I endured scholastic challenges and the embarrassment and scrutiny that came with being suspended from my previous college. It was hard, but I made it to the end of my challenge with sweat, tears, and all! I earned my bachelor's degree and graduated with honors. Graduating from Temple University is one of my proudest moments because even though I went down the wrong path and screwed up many things in my life up to that point, I was able to turn things around for the good of my purpose by accepting the challenge of change and breaking down the walls and mind-grenades that tried to deter me and convince me that I was a failure that didn't deserve a second chance. I was faced with many obstacles, but I knocked some of them down and went over or around others to complete my challenge and reach my goal. On a sunny September afternoon, I walked onto the stage and received my degree as my parents, brother, and future husband looked on.

Challenges are meant to make us better – not break us. As you decide you want to live a life ignited, you have to ignite your inner fuse and resolve to take on the challenge of change. Don't get scared because of the season of discomfort. Get excited about the doors that are about to be opened and think about the things you are going to accomplish when you complete your challenge. Embrace and endure your challenge of change knowing that your life ignited is waiting at the end of your challenge.

Consistency of Change

To see positive change that ultimately leads to sustainable growth in your life, your commitment to change has to be consistent. When change is consistent, it happens every day, on purpose, on schedule. It is not by happenstance. When you decide you want to improve your overall quality of living or make yourself a better version of yourself, you have to decide to approach every day with your goals and vision top of mind. You must do something each day that is consistent with your plan and your purpose. You cannot finish any type of project if you only work on it when the mood hits you or whenever you feel like it. When you work in that way, it's hard to accomplish or complete anything. If you are not consistent in your approach to changing and becoming a better person, you'll find yourself back where you started working on yet another approach to living a life ignited—only to find little success in that strategy also. Until you are consistently working towards your purpose, you will not see the results you crave.

Consistency of change means your actions are in line with the person you want to become or the things you want to accomplish. As Stephen Covey, author of *The 7 Habits of Highly Effective People*, suggests, when you begin with the end in mind, you consistently work towards your ending. You know where you are going and your everyday actions are consistent with that vision. Change is not a part-time job. Change is not something you pull off the shelf when you feel like it and put back when you don't want to play with it anymore.

If you are serious about wanting to accomplish your goals, rising above your current situation, and working to thrive and not just survive, you need to be consistent with the changes you make in your life. You have to put in the necessary work on a daily basis to see the change in your life that you desire. You cannot be lazy with your dreams. Laziness, lack of commitment, and inconsistency are sure ways to keep yourself far away from your appointed position of prosperity - and your life ignited.

Work every day to be the person you want to be. Work every day to be the person you were meant to be. Work every day to be the person you know you can be. Consistently work every day to be the person you deserve to be!

The secret of success is consistency of purpose.
- Benjamin Disraeli

When you consistently show the world you want to be better, the world around you will get better—and you will start to see a positive shift in your life. The circumstances around you will not dictate your decisions any longer. Instead, you will begin to dictate the circumstances around you simply by the consistent changes you are making in both your mind and in your actions.

Light your inner fuse and commit to change. Devote your actions and energy to your purpose. Understand that change will be challenging. There will be obstacles along in your path. As you meet those obstacles head on, find creative ways to overcome them. Be open-minded and resourceful. And as you defeat obstacles and complete the challenges, be consistent. Keep up the good work and do not fall back into patterns of monotony or laziness. Sustain your successes with infinite consistency and continue to journey towards living your life ignited.

GET RID OF BAD
RELATIONSHIPS

Let us strip off every weight that slows us down.
- Hebrews 12:2

THE PEOPLE AND THINGS YOU are in relationship with
affect and impact your ability to live a life ignited.
They either help elevate you to firework status or hold you back
and keep you from achieving your goals. Too many of us are in
relationships with people or things that have never been good
for us, will never be good for us, and will be the end of us if
we continue to stay bound to those relationships.

A relationship is the way in which you are connected to
someone or something. People can have relationships with
food, alcohol, drugs, the Internet, video games, social media,
groups, organizations, and ideologies. For example, does your
obsession (relationship) with shopping keep you from staying
on a budget, which ultimately keeps you from your goal of

financial freedom or paying your bills on time? Do you find yourself on Facebook perusing statuses when you really should be studying, writing, or spending time with your spouse who already feels neglected? Is your relationship with your cell phone keeping you from being present in the moment with your children because you are preoccupied with taking selfies or playing games? Does your relationship with junk food and sweets keep you from living the healthy lifestyle your doctor has advised?

Relationships with "things" can be just as harmful as relationships with people.

I'm sure you've seen a glimpse of one of the many shows on television about extreme hoarding. Extreme hoarding is the excessive acquisition of and inability or unwillingness to get rid of large amounts of stuff, mostly junk and trash that cover a person's home and space from top to bottom. This causes high levels of distress and this condition impairs a person's judgment. Hoarders have strong emotional relationships with their "stuff". When anyone touches their stuff or threatens to remove any of it, hoarders typically become upset, irate, and sometimes physically violent. Many underlying issues such as guilt, sorrow, and hurt, cause people to start hoarding things, but ultimately the relationships with their stuff are outward expressions of that internal pain.

You may not be an extreme hoarder who refuses to throw away stuff and declutter things in your home, but you may be holding on to unhealthy relationships that have little or no value to your life. These relationships are merely clutter.

They cloud your judgment and stifle your success. Even though you know these relationships are not good for you, you hold on to them anyway. The idea of severing these relationships makes you uneasy and uncomfortable—and sometimes a little angry and defensive—but if you want to live your life ignited, cleaning up or throwing out some of your relationships is a must! You may not be living a life ignited right now because you are in a relationship with someone or something that is holding you back from your greatness. It's time to become aware of your surroundings and see how the people, places, and things in your life either help ignite your fuse or keep you below the firework status you deserve.

> *You hang out with coconuts, you get nowhere.*
> *They're eleven, eleven. You hang out with nice people,*
> *you get nice friends, y'understand? You hang out with*
> *smart people, you get smart friends. You hang out with*
> *yo-yo people, you get yo-yo friends! Y'see, it's simple*
> *mathematics.*
> *- Rocky*

When you commit to igniting your inner fuse, you must take a good look at your relationships and the company you are keeping. Before we go any further, please understand that you will have relationships with people and things that are absolutely not aligned with your goals and dreams. And that's okay—as long as the relationships do not threaten YOUR ability to ignite your fuse and move forward with your goals. However, if you are in a relationship that causes you to compromise your values, integrity, or ability to live a life ignited, you need to check that relationship because it's not a good relationship for you to be in.

A good relationship plays in harmony with your goals and will naturally support, encourage, and respect your journey. Good relationships are grounded in truth and respect, and they never compromise your purpose. If a relationship is in your best interest, it will elevate you -and even serve as a catalyst as it propels you further toward your desires. You know you are in a good relationship when you are a better person because of that person or thing's presence in your life. The support and encouragement you get from good relationships gives you the necessary confidence for traveling on your journey. If your goal is to go back to school and earn an advanced degree, you need relationships that will foster an environment of support and motivation. Good relationships will make sure you are never late for class and will encourage you to study and get your assignments done. They will lift you up when you feel like you want to quit and provide a support climate of growth and progress. When the relationships in your life work in tandem with your efforts to ignite your inner fuse and follow your dreams, you know you are in a good relationship. Even with transition and changes you start to make in your life, good relationships will not frown upon you for wanting to do better and reach an ignited status in your life. They will salute your efforts and celebrate you along the way – even when they don't quite understand your journey. Good relationships will ride with you, pushing and encouraging you through the best and toughest of times.

The opposite of a good relationship are relationships that block a dream (BAD). If a relationship keeps you stagnant and prevents you from pursuing your passions and living a life ignited, then you are in a BAD relationship. BAD relationships serve no purpose in your journey to live your life ignited. If a relationship is moving left, and your dreams and desires are turning right, how will the relationship assist you in realizing your dreams and accomplishing your goals? That sounds more like tug-of-war, and not a good relationship to be in. If you believe you can do anything you set your mind to, but someone is telling you that you'll never be anything or something is preventing you from living to your fullest potential, why are you in that relationship? If the relationship is the reason why you have disconnected your passion from your purpose, ask yourself why you are in it.

> *Life is partly what we make it, and partly what it is*
> *made by the friends we choose.*
> *- Tennessee Williams*

I was in a BAD relationship with a guy in college. I couldn't see it while I was in it, but after we broke up, I realized that many of my problems were rooted in that relationship. I am not blaming him. I take full ownership for my actions and choices, and I'm clear that being in that relationship was a BAD choice that I made. I was spending all my time chasing this guy - spending less time doing class work and assignments. I was totally wrapped up in the relationship. I lost sight of my goals; I rarely studied and I failed or barely passed most of my classes. This toxic relationship was wearing on my academics and my emotions. At some point, I looked at the relationship and thought, *"Why am I here?"* I thought about all the negatives that were clouding my judgment and sensibility and made the decision to move on with my life – without him. After the breakup, I took control of my goals again and started to focus on what was important for me.

Until you get rid of toxic relationships in your life, you will continue to be held back. Toxic relationships are shackles keeping you in your RUT. So long as you are chained to them, it's difficult to pursue your passion and reach your goals. One BAD relationship can hold you captive and keep you from your goals, dreams, and the life you crave - forever.

Many people are in relationships that will never allow them to realize their full potential. My heart aches for those I've seen settle for BAD relationships and live years, decades, and even lifetimes of mediocrity and unhappiness. They gave up on what they wanted most and settled for relationships that crushed and, in some cases, killed their dreams.

The good news about toxic relationships and their shackles is that you hold the key to the shackles. By making good choices, you can set yourself free. To free yourself from BAD relationships, start by taking a long, hard, and honest look at the relationships affecting your life's choices, ask important questions about those relationships, give honest answers, and begin to make smart decisions about the future of those relationships.

> *Each relationship nurtures a strength or weakness*
> *within you.*
> *- Mike Murdock*

You have to make aggressive and dream-friendly decisions about your relationships. Don't stick around, believing in the fantasy that the relationship will miraculously turn in your favor. Don't settle for what you have and give up on what you really want. When you settle or give up, you never lose the weight, you never gain the financial freedom, you never get the diploma or degree, you never beat the addiction, and you never feel fulfilled in romantic relationships. Don't settle for mediocrity. A critical step in the journey of living a life ignited is making smart decisions about your relationships. Ignite your inner fuse and set yourself free from BAD relationships so you can soar toward the life you know you deserve to live.

Why are you letting this person, place or thing, block your blessings?

I am not suggesting that relationships be perfect. That's just unrealistic. I understand that people are flawed. I am flawed. You are flawed. Our human nature is that we are flawed, so naturally relationships will be flawed. However, through the midst of the imperfections, you should have a reasonable expectation and minimum standard that the relationships in your life will serve your purpose as you pursue it with passion. If you find that your relationships make it difficult for you to press on, follow your path, or reach your goals, you need to think about why you are allowing these relationships to take up space and suck up energy in your life.

I had to part ways with a friend who I thought would be in my life forever. For years, I pretended the relationship was not toxic and ignored all the signs of a BAD relationship. At some point, I faced the reality that the relationship was dragging me down. Leaving it behind was hard. I missed my friend. My heart was heavy for a while, but my head knew the negative energy and constant bickering was unhealthy, unproductive, and unnecessary. Since the issues we had could not be resolved, I chose to go my separate way. I still miss her at times, but I am proud of the choice I made. I'm a better woman because I chose peace and progress over chaos and shackles. I can say with a hundred percent confidence that both of our lives were better in the long run. Leaving that toxic relationship created space in my life for new, healthy friendships that cultivate an atmosphere of fun, growth, love, and support.

Another BAD relationship that almost killed me was my relationship with food! Yes, food - specifically foods with high sodium levels. *You do know that you have a relationship with food? Don't you?* Several cardio exams revealed that I have a high sensitivity to. My cardiologist told me to change my diet—or risk having a stroke or a heart attack due to high blood pressure (hypertension)—but it wasn't enough to scare me straight. I like to eat, and I loved salty foods. At the time I thought food tastes so much better with salty spices and sauces. So, I continued to eat what I wanted and ignored the advice of my cardiologist—until I had a medical scare and suffered from hypertension retinopathy. Hypertension retinopathy is a condition suffered when the blood vessels in your eyes get overworked, because of high blood pressure, and stop working. Yup, I lost part of my vision. When I lost part of my vision in the upper left quadrant of my right eye, I realized that I was in a BAD relationship with salt and food. I was going to die of a stroke or a heart attack or go completely blind if I didn't change something quickly. I immediately got out of that BAD relationship with salt. I changed my diet and still to this day, I work every day to prevent any more scary blood pressure-induced health and life threatening episodes.

Even when it feels so good and tastes so delicious, your BAD relationships can be deadly. You have to ask yourself if the BAD relationship is worth the risk.

Are you willing to kill your dreams, or die, for that bad relationship?

If you are in a relationship that is blocking your blessing and keeping you from personal greatness, don't lose yourself in that relationship. Don't lose sight (literally, like me) of your goals and dreams. If you are in a BAD relationship, the time is now to do something about it – change it, revive it if there is still life left, or simply let it go.

A friend is one that knows you as you are, understands where you have been, accepts what you have become, and still, gently allows you to grow.
- William Shakespeare

First, assess the relationships in your life and how they interact with the goals you want to achieve. List the top ten relationships in your life. You can do it below or make a list on a separate piece of paper. Since this list is private, I suggest writing on a separate piece of paper. To help you determine who you spend your time with and how you spend your time, here are a few ideas to help you start creating your list:

- *Who and what do you spend most of your time with?*
- *Who and what are vital parts of your journey?*
- *Do you spend a lot of time on Facebook or play Candy Crush or other games on your phone or computer? List them. You are in relationship with them.*
- *Do you watch a lot of TV? If so, list the shows you watch faithfully every week.*
- *Who are the people or things that most influence your life decisions (both good and bad)?*

This list should include coworkers, family, friends, things, and places. Any relationship that plays some sort of role in your ability to progress in the direction of your dreams should be on this list.

1. _____
2. _____
3. _____
4. _____
5. _____
6. _____
7. _____
8. _____
9. _____
10. _____

Once you have this list compiled, I want you to look at each line item and answer the following questions.

- *Is this relationship important to me? Explain.*

- *Is this a good relationship? Explain.*
- *Is this a BAD relationship? Explain.*
- *How does this relationship support my journey to living a life ignited?*
- *How does this relationship keep me from living a life ignited?*
- *What are the opportunities for me to improve this relationship so that it is more of an asset than a liability?*
- *What are the advantages and disadvantages of this relationship?*
- *If this relationship disappeared tomorrow, how would my life be impacted?*

Answer honestly. Your answers will allow you to start making smart decisions when it comes to managing and prioritizing the relationships in your life. Recognize the BAD relationships in your life—and decide whether you need to release them or make corrections to the connections. Some relationships can be fixed. If you can right the wrongs in your BAD relationships, definitely work to keep the relationship together. However, if the relationship will continue to be unhealthy and prevent you from pursuing your life ignited, you've got to let it go!

Aggressively manage the BAD relationships in your life. Be fearless about who and what you are in relationships with. Use your head and not your heart to make smart choices. Your relationships can be the difference between a life ignited or the death of a dream.

FEAR LESS AND EXERCISE YOUR FAITH MORE

Everything you want is on the other side of fear.
—Jack Canfield

I LEARNED VERY EARLY IN MY adult life that, just like BAD relationships, fear is a dream blocker. If you succumb to its false threats of failure, you will be too scared to journey down your path toward your life ignited. When you give in to fear, you make excuses, justify your mediocre or stagnant behavior, and convince yourself that where you are is okay. Fear is one of the most powerful tools of the mind. Fear is crippling. Fear creates an immobilizing spirit in your mind and body. Having a fearful mind-set paralyzes your passion for your purpose. Fear focuses on the risk of failure if you take action toward your goals and desires. Fear convinces you that you are better off staying in your comfort zone where it feels stable, cozy, and familiar. Fear tells you that if you rock the boat, you just might sink.

> *How can you live a life of purpose on purpose with passion if you are fearful of moving toward your goals and dreams?*

I used to be afraid of standing in my power, owning my greatness, and living my life ignited. I always focused on the possibilities of failure. On more than one occasion, I talked myself out of pursuing my passions. Being afraid to stand up for myself, ask for what I want, step out the box, and be uniquely wonderful (the way God made me) has cost me time, energy, money, joy, and happiness.

> *What has fear cost you?*

At some point, I became sick and tired of being so darn fearful all the time. Letting fear control my every move was holding me back. When I'd had enough, I took action. I decided to fear "less", and when I did start to fear less, doors began to open and my life began to change.

> *When I let go of fear, I was like a rocket propelled to the open air of abundance and prosperity.*

> *I began to experience my appointed position of prosperity where I always knew I was meant to reign.*

After earning my bachelor's degree from Temple, I continued to work fulltime for a private financial-services software company. Prior to my fulltime position with the company, I was selected to work as an intern. I was lucky to have been selected for the internship because Sungard Trading Systems had never hired an intern from Temple University before. All of their interns were students at Drexel University, the alma mater of many of its employees. To my delight, when I interviewed for the internship, they offered me the internship on the spot.

I stood out as a top performer. I impressed the management team with my work ethic, my productivity, and my ability to learn new things quickly. The six-month internship was so successful that I was offered a full-time job as a product analyst. I hadn't even graduated from college yet, and I had a big-girl job that was paying me big-girl money. I was used to earning minimum wage at the mall, and here at Sungard, my starting salary was $27,000 a year. Talk about a come up! I had health and dental benefits and a tuition-reimbursement benefit that gave me the financial support I needed to continue to go to school part-time in the evenings while working full-time during the day. It was an exciting time in my life. At twenty-one, I was young, hopeful, and making big strides in my professional and personal lives. I even purchased my first home during that time.

Over the next two years, I showed Sungard what I was really made of - and upper management and my peers took notice of my hard work and dedication to the company. I was rewarded with opportunities to travel and meet clients, and work with consultants in our various European offices. I traveled to London, Rome, and Zurich for weeks at a time working, touring, and learning so much about myself - and the world.

When I graduated from Temple with my Bachelor's in Business Administration/Finance degree, the company promoted me to a Product Manager. My new title came with a salary of $36,000 a year. Although I was happy that the managers thought enough of me to promote me, I was not happy with the salary I was offered because I knew the starting salary for the position was close to $45,000 (remember, this was back in the mid 90's and I was barely 21 years old). I'd proven myself to the company, and I was a valued team member who my peers respected. *Why wasn't I being paid the minimum starting salary for the job I was doing and excelling in?* I would come home and tell my boyfriend (now my husband) how pissed I was that I wasn't being paid what I should be paid.

He would always ask, "Why don't you tell them you want a raise?"

I would always say, "No! I can't do that. They'll get mad at me, and I'll lose my job."

With each passing month, I became more frustrated about my salary. We were hiring new employees, and I knew they were making more money than I was. I was even training and mentoring a few of the new hires. I knew I had several options: I could say nothing, continue to be mad about this issue, and continue to work with a chip on my shoulder. I could look for a new job where I would be paid according to my value, or I could go to the management team and ask for a raise. I really loved my job, and I did not want to look for another one, but I was too afraid to ask for a raise, so I worked with a chip on my shoulder for months.

You have not 'cause you ask not.

-Rhonda Kinard

Being a disgruntled employee takes a lot of effort and negative energy. I was done carrying the weight of the "attitude chip" on my shoulder. I stopped focusing on my fears and started focusing on my purpose and the vision I had for my life. I turned my attention to all the positive things that could happen if I asked for a raise and actually got it. I would be able to pay my bills and save more money each month. I would be able to invest in the company's 401(k). I would be able to buy things I wanted and not just what I needed all the time. I'd be able to accelerate my student loan payments. I'd always had a special place in my heart for St. Jude's Children Hospital - more money would allow me to start philanthropic efforts and donate to the hospital and help the sick kids and their families. And above all, I would feel more fulfilled and appreciated for the job I was doing if I knew I was being compensated fairly. This whole fear thing had gotten old. If I wanted more, I had to get up, change my mind-set, and stop letting fear control me. I had to go ask for a raise. And that's exactly what I did.

One week before my twenty-third birthday, I got up from my desk and headed over to the office of Thomas Gambino, one of the Senior Vice Presidents at Sungard. I gently knocked on his open door and asked if he had a minute to talk. He invited me in and motioned for me to sit. After we got a few courtesies out of the way, I told him how I thought I deserved a raise. My heart was racing, and I started feeling hot and anxious, as we sat watching me speak.

Despite how nervous I felt, I worked through the fear. I did not let it keep me from having that important conversation with Tom. I looked him directly in the eye and told him I loved my job, but based on my performance and industry standards, I felt I was not being paid appropriately.

He listened attentively, wearing a poker face, as I spoke. After I stepped down off my soapbox, Tom said, "So what do you think we should pay you?"

Even though I had two years of experience with the company and worked hard every day to make the clients and my coworkers happy, I felt as though I should be conservative with my response. I didn't want to push it. I said, "I think I should make $45,000 a year."

He nodded slowly and explained that he needed to consult with a few other senior managers. He looked at a calendar and then looked back at me. "Is it okay if I get back to you in one week?"

I said, "Sure. One week from today is my birthday."

We thanked each other and cordially ended the meeting with smiles. A sense of pride overcame me when I walked out of his office. I didn't let fear keep me from pursuing something that I knew was rightfully mine. It felt good to be bold and brave!

The next day, Tom was already there when I got to work. When he saw me, he motioned for me to come into his office. *Oh my gosh! It's only been one day since we spoke. This is not good.* I walked into his office and took a seat.

As soon as I sat down, Tom looked at me with a grin and said, "Rhonda, you're right! You are underpaid! However, when

I spoke to my team of managers, they didn't think we should pay you $45,000 a year for the job you do."

My heart immediately sank, and I felt a sense of agitation starting to overcome me. *What does he mean I'm not worth $45,000 year?*

He said, "Collectively, we agree that your new salary, effective today, is $50,000 a year, with a bonus in appreciation for all the hard work you've done up to this point. The way we see it is if we don't pay you what you're worth, someone else will. What do you think about that?"

I could barely contain my excitement. I was so happy to hear these words. I told him the offer was more than fair—and that I was happy with it.

After going over the next steps, we shook hands, smiled at one another, and I walked out of his office. I was intoxicated with joy. I felt so good. That was one of the best days of my life—not because I got a raise—because a braver and more confident version of me was unleashed! The new audacious and more optimistic version of me was born a week before my twenty-third birthday.

When I thought of all the time I wasted being afraid and full of fear, I wanted to slap myself. Fear convinced me that I should have played it safe, sat down, shut up, and been grateful for the salary I was getting. But when I put fear to the side, I got more than I ever imagined. My life was positively affected by the decision to take executive control away from fear.

"Fire Fear as your CEO"
- Darnyelle A. Jervey

49

After getting the raise, I continued to fear less at work. It was definitely a confidence booster. Even in my personal life, I began to walk more confidently and boldly. I made aggressive goals, and I created high standards for the type of woman I wanted to be. Fear did not hinder my decisions any longer. Fear did not manage me; I managed my fears. Knowing the risks of failure and rejection as I moved toward living my life ignited didn't stifle or scare me. I moved forward anyway. Sometimes I was rejected; I didn't always get the "yes" I wanted and there were times when doors didn't open. But fear did not keep me from asking or pulling on the knob. When I failed, I didn't give up. I learned from the experience, got up, dusted myself off, and kept going. Not being afraid allowed me to keep going, stand my ground, and consistently keep moving towards my purpose.

> *You can conquer almost any fear if you will only*
> *make up your mind to do so. For remember, fear doesn't*
> *exist anywhere except in the mind.*
> *- Dale Carnegie*

In 2006, my husband and I decided to start investing in real estate. We'd just started our family (my son was a year old), and we decided it was time to start laying the financial foundation for our children and the future of our family. We were excited to begin a new unknown adventure together. We shared our good news with some friends. They had expressed interest in being real estate investors, too, but they had not put a plan in motion to make it happen.

They said, "What if your tenants don't pay the rent? What if you flip a house, but it doesn't sell? Is all your money going to be tied up in a house that may not make any profit?" The wife asked question after question. Each question highlighted the negative outcome that could possibly occur from taking a risk and investing in real estate. This couple had aspirations of investing in real estate too, but they were too scared to take the risk. When she thought about investing—or any financial venture—she focused on all the ways they could fail, crash, or burn.

When my husband and I got into real estate, we were aware of the risks. We were a little nervous about them, but we were more excited about all the ways we could succeed and prosper in a lucrative and profitable business. We purchased several houses, and based on our fiscal goals, we either provided quality housing for tenants or served the community by revitalizing dilapidated homes in low-income areas that were eventually sold to families who otherwise would not have been able to afford a fully renovated home. When we successfully flipped houses, we made the dream of homeownership a reality for others. Not only did we serve communities, but the risks we took turned into a profitable business and created opportunities for our children they would not have if we were too full of fear to step out of our comfort zones.

Whose blessing are you blocking because you are too afraid to step into your greatness?

When you live a life ignited, it is not that you're without fear. I'd be lying if said I didn't feel fear about taking risks and trying new things. You have to be superhuman or immortal not to get scared and feel fear sometimes. I'm not suggesting that you walk around fearless when, in actuality, a little fear is a good thing. But in order to move successfully toward your goals and dreams, you cannot let fear hijack your purpose and passion. If you do, you'll come to a grinding halt and never reach the ignited status that you deserve and crave.

You gain strength, courage, and confidence by each experience in which you really stop to look fear in the face. You are able to say to yourself, "I have lived through this horror. I can take the next thing that comes along." You must do the thing you think you cannot do.- Eleanor Roosevelt

I am suggesting that you fear less and exercise your faith more! Replace fear with faith. Where fear is paralyzing and unfit in the life of someone who is trying to live a life ignited, faith is the motivating catalyst that encourages you to pursue your purpose with passion despite your perceptions of risk and negative outcomes. Just like fear, faith is based on the unknown.

Faith is the confidence that what we hope for will actually happen; it gives us assurance about things we cannot see
- Hebrews 11:1

Don't let fear convince you that your comfort zone is your home. Take risks and step out in faith. Faith is optimism and expectation of good things. Exercise your faith—and believe you can achieve greatness in your life. Know that you are ready to journey toward your life ignited. Trust that you will realize your dreams and goals with focus, faith, and determination.

Much of the success I have had in professional ventures is attributed to the fact that I stepped out in faith and believed that great things would happen—even when I had no idea how the good thing was going to happen because everything and everyone around me tried to convince me that what I was doing was a bad idea and that nothing good would come of it.

Some people thought my marriage would not last. But, I had faith in my husband, and when he was broke as a joke with no money and a crappy job, I knew he would rise out of darkness and be a man of greatness. People underestimated him, me, and us. Boy, were the unfaithful, fearful, naysayers, and haters wrong. Today, we stand together as best friends, business partners, lovers, and parents of two wonderful children. Many of the people who doubted us and spoke darkness and failure upon my marriage are divorced, unhappy, broke, busted, and disgusted. Their fears did not deter me. Faith led me down this path, and I am so thankful that I exercised faith all the times I did.

Let faith guide you and keep you. Be bold and fear less as you step out of your comfort zone. With faith, you are unstoppable. Believe in all that you dream of—and in all that you work for— and go after your purpose with passion. Nothing can stop a person who is faithful, passionate, and determined to succeed. Ignite your inner fuse and let faith lead you to your life ignited.

BOLDNESS, BOUNDARIES, AND SELF-LOVE

Boundaries: the key to confidence,
calm, and self-control.
—Rokelle Lerner

I WORKED AT SUNGARD FOR FIVE years before I started looking for a new job. It was time to move on from Sungard once I got engaged. I knew that once I was married, I wanted to start a family. I didn't want to travel for work once I became a wife and a mother. It was important to have a good work-life harmony that allowed me to work hard during the day and then go home and be the wife and mother I needed to be for my family. I also needed a little relaxation time. Sungard was flexible, but traveling out of the country was a job requirement. Since I did not want to compromise my family life for work, I decided to get a new job where I could meet and manage my work-life harmony goals.

It didn't take me very long to find a new job. I interviewed for a Quality Assurance Analyst position at ING. ING (now Voya Financial) was a financial-services company located about twenty-five miles outside of Philadelphia. I interviewed with the Director of Quality Assurance, Teresa Christensen. She was smart, very nice, and shared many of my ideas regarding software testing and the workplace in general.

During my interview with Teresa, I made it very clear that work-life harmony was important to me. I went on to say that even though I didn't have children at the time—and I wasn't quite married yet—I still valued the opportunity to leave work at a reasonable hour. I told her I liked to leave work at four o'clock (which was the time I was leaving Sungard every day). Leaving work at that time, and not having to travel abroad for work, allowed me to enjoy my life outside of work and gave me the needed time to rejuvenate and recharge my batteries for the next workday. I stressed how important work-life harmony was to me and explained how it was the primary reason I was leaving Sungard – I didn't want to travel, work late, and compromise my life at home. I asked if my work-life harmony goals would be a problem at ING. To my delight, she agreed that work-life harmony is important and said that my scheduling requests would not be a problem. The rest of the interview went well, and just like my SunGard interview, I was hired on the spot. Once I received the offer letter in the mail, I happily accepted it. ING provided professional growth, great benefits, a good salary, a fun environment, and great coworkers. It was the perfect fit for the lifestyle I wanted live. I gave my two weeks' notice to SunGard and started in my new role at ING three weeks later.

For the first two weeks I worked at ING, everything was going great. My coworkers were nice, and the work was new and interesting. At three o'clock on the Thursday of my second week, one of the managers in my department made an announcement that my team would be doing a quick stress test. The manager, Bonnie, walked around and announced that the stress test would begin as soon as she coordinated a few things with our IT department since they would be overseeing the stress test.

Even though nothing in the QA and software testing world is ever quick, I thought I would be able to complete it before I left at four o'clock. By 3:30, we still had not started the stress test. When we still hadn't started the stress test at four o'clock, I wrapped up the work I was doing, packed my bag, and started toward the stairwell. I looked over at my team leader, Lori, and said "Have a good evening." I then said good-bye to my other coworkers.

Lori smiled and said, "You too."

My coworkers were shocked that I was leaving before the stress test started. A few of them made comments under their breath, but I could still hear them.

As I got to the stairwell, Bonnie turned the corner and said, "Where are you going?"

"I'm leaving for the day, Bonnie," I said calmly.

She replied in a stern voice, saying, "But we have a stress test to do."

I replied, "I know, but it's time for me to leave, Bonnie."

There was a moment of awkward silence. She looked at me, and I looked at her.

I excused myself, said good-bye to everyone again, and left the building. I drove home and enjoyed a relaxing evening with my fiancé.

Could I have stayed past four and completed the stress test? Sure. But this was about more than just staying after four. It was about getting management to respect my boundaries early in the work relationship. If I'd walked back to my desk, sat around, and waited for the stress test to start when Bonnie confronted me, I would've never been able to get my team and the managers to respect my desired schedule. Having work-life harmony was the primary reason I decided to work at ING. If I compromised that benefit early on, it would be almost impossible to get managers to respect my schedule—or me—in the future.

When I got to work the next day, I was pretty certain there would be some backlash. When I logged into my computer, the first thing I did was check my e-mail. To my shock, there was no nasty-gram (aka reprimanding e-mail) there.

As people started to arrive to work, I heard that Bonnie did complain to Teresa about my actions. I waited patiently for them to arrive, knowing I was most likely going to have to defend my actions to them.

When Bonnie and Teresa got to work, there was no mention of me leaving before the stress test. I couldn't believe it. I was ready to defend my actions, but I never had to. Neither of them mentioned the incident. I worked at ING for more than five years without any other incidents. I got married and gave birth to my children while I worked for ING. It was a great company to work for. I made new friends, matured as a professional, contributed to the success of my team, and won awards for my service and skills—all while never working past four o'clock.

I was aware that walking out that day was a bold move. I knew the risks, but I stood my ground. Being bold and uncompromising about my needs worked in my favor that day. My unwavering actions allowed me to enjoy a good work-life harmony while I was employed at ING.

Choose to be pro-active, assertive and self-defining.
- Bryant McGill

When you live your life ignited, you have to be bold. There will always be people who want you to put your goals and dreams on the back burner while they push their own agendas. The direction of the wind may shift and require you to adjust your sail, but the purpose of your journey should never sink.

When you live a life ignited, dreams deferred are not an option. I have friends who hate their jobs. They are overworked and underpaid because they lack boldness. Too scared to lose their jobs, they never stand up for themselves or express their needs or wants to their bosses. I know that feeling. I've been in those stilettos and walked in those shoes - but as long as you lack the ability to fight for your dreams, you will never live your life ignited. You cannot pursue your passions if you are too afraid to confront any roadblocks and obstacles in your path.

The boundary to what we can accept is the boundary
to our freedom.
- Tara Brach

My experience has been that people are very responsive when you tell them your needs and requirements. In most cases, telling people what you desire helps them work better with you because it gives them guidelines and protocols to follow with you. Relationships are better when people know where you stand and how you feel about certain issues and situations.

When I met potential real estate clients who are looking to buy or sell a home, I briefly introduced myself and then I start the business portion of my presentation by saying, *"Now, let me tell you how I work."* It is important that my clients know how I operate – how I do business. They need to understand how I communicate, negotiate, and work throughout the process of helping them buy or sell a home. Since I give them all the information upfront, they have the option to say, "This woman is crazy. No, thank you!", and choose not to do business with me. Or they could say, "This all sounds great. Let's do this!" I am okay with either decision my potential clients make. I have boundaries. I run my business with consistency of my message and the boundaries that I work within. I'm such a stickler about boundaries in my business because when I was operating without them, I ended up in difficult situations, with houses that did not sell and unhappy buyers and sellers when their deals fell apart.

> *"No" is a complete sentence.*
> *- Anne Lamott*

> *The difference between successful people and really*
> *successful people is that really successful people say 'No'*
> *to almost everything.*
> *- Warren Buffet*

Boundaries are important for reaching your goals and living your life ignited. Setting and sticking to your boundaries requires you to be bold. Understand that being bold is not the same as being rude or disrespectful. Being bold is an attribute; it is a badge of honor and self-respect. When you are bold, you are courageous—not hesitant—and you fear less and exercise your faith more. People on the other side of your bold acts will try to make you think you are being rude, but that's because most people live their lives unignited, are passive aggressive, and never really grab the bull by the horns and go for what they want. When you stand up for yourself or act with boldness, people tend to misconstrue this for arrogance or rudeness, but it's absolutely not either. Being bold allows you to set boundaries and demand levels of respect that others cannot fathom because they are full of fear or are—worst of all—people pleasers.

> *It is necessary, and even vital, to set standards for*
> *your life and the people you allow in it.*
> *- Mandy Hale*

Bold boundaries are necessary if you plan to ignite your inner fuse and pursue your purpose with passion. How will people know how to treat and handle you if you do not set boundaries and tell them how you work? Furniture, appliances, and cars come with instructions; you have to come with instructions, too. You need to provide a set of rules for others to follow. Create bold boundaries and let the world know how you work. Your boundaries are your how-to guide. Tell people how things will operate in your space. If you do not tell people how you work, they will create their own sets of instructions for your life, and most likely, those instructions will not be aligned with your purpose.

It's important to maintain a certain level of control in all aspects of your life and boundaries allow you to do just that. Many people have let people, places, and things come into their spaces and run amuck. They have not told people how they work. Too scared or afraid to honor themselves first, they put up with other people's shenanigans, let people talk them out of their dreams, and let useless and negative people take up precious space around them. Be bold about your boundaries. If something or someone is going against your beliefs, goals, or moral fabric, you have to pump the brakes and stand up for yourself. Set bold boundaries and then have faith that those boundaries will serve you as you pursue your purpose with passion.

Bold boundaries aren't just for other people to know how you work. These boundaries also remind you how you work. They keep you focused on your goals and dreams. Boundaries help keep you from going out of bounds. I have boundaries for my life, and there are some things I'm just not going to do because they are unproductive and will only hinder my progress in reaching my goals. Bold boundaries make a statement about the type of person you are and the type of life you want to live.

*Bold boundaries are an outward expression of your
morals, integrity, and innermost values.*

The various times my life was in disarray, it was mainly because of the lack of boundaries in my life. I had to look at myself, reflect on my poor choices, and really understand what was going on with me. I had to ask myself tough questions. Why was I reckless and living without boundaries? Why was I veering off my course? Why was I so scared of upsetting people? I grew up with strong morals and values; why wasn't I acting like I had some home training and a good upbringing?

The lack of boldness and boundaries was a definite issue in my life, but I wasn't bold enough to create boundaries because I didn't have self-love. I was not in love with myself. I saw myself through the eyes of others, and I wanted to please everyone. I disregarded my code of ethics, and I basically did whatever it took to make everyone else happy. The problem with trying to make everyone happy is that it's impossible to make every person happy at all times. Since I looked at myself through the eyes of others all the time, I was vulnerable. And vulnerability coupled with no self-love equals weakness. I was too weak and afraid to set bold boundaries in my life.

It took years of growth, maturity, and self-awareness to realize that I did not truly love myself. I had to learn to love myself. I had to learn how to be comfortable in my own skin. I figured out through many life experiences that you cannot please people. There will always be someone who does not like something you do or say. There will always be someone who disagrees with you or thinks you are strange, ugly, stupid, or even uneducated.

I had to learn that it's okay if others think negatively
of me or do not understand me fully. I had to learn that
my value is not connected to other's people's ideas of who
I am or what I am doing.

Self-love is loving yourself enough to be who you are and being courageous enough to stand firm in what makes you who you are. Self-love is understanding that you cannot manage people's expectations of you. Self-love is not giving into temptations that disrupt your journey and prevent you from pursuing your purpose with passion. Self-love is believing that you are unique, explosive, and powerful—like a firework. Do not look at your life through the eyes of others. Do not depend on others for your happiness. Learn to appreciate everything about who you are and how God made you. Love yourself enough to set boundaries that help you improve your quality of life.

To live a life ignited, YOU must believe in the power you possess to walk in your power and thrive in life. Stop looking for acceptance from others. God didn't need approval from anybody when he made you perfect in his sight. Why do you think you need the approval of others as you pursue your purpose with passion? Be brave enough to have dreams of your own. Loving yourself unconditionally means being faithful and honest with yourself—no matter what others think or say about you.

See your potential from the vision of how your life will be once you start to live your life ignited. Create bold boundaries that you live by—and demand that others respect your boundaries. It's okay if not everyone likes you or your boundaries. Be bold and love what you bring to the table.

Your unique chemistry and past experiences—both good and bad—make you valuable, important, and beautiful from the inside out. Embody what makes you special. Fall in love with yourself. Travel boldly toward your destiny. Your journey and your decisions don't need to be approved, qualified, or accepted by anyone else. Ignite your inner fuse, follow your heart, know that you are enough, and create boundaries that will allow you to live your best life—your life ignited.

CRAFT YOUR WORLD

Create the highest, grandest vision possible for your
life because you become what you believe.
—Oprah Winfrey

THIS IS THE FUN PART -crafting your world. At the beginning of this book, I shared what differentiates someone living a life ignited from a wishful daydreamer – and that is action. It's time to take action and craft a new world that will support and encourage you to ignite your inner fuse and start living your life ignited.

Moving forward, your life should not look or feel like it did before you read this book. You are about to shake things up—and that's a great thing that you should be really excited about. Remember those questions from the Introduction, let's revisit them.

Take a few moments, close your eyes, and luxuriate in the vision you have for your life. What will your life look like when you expose your greatness within, reach your goals, and accomplish your dreams?

> *What does that picture look like?*
> *What do you look like?*
> *What are you doing?*
> *Where are you?*
> *How do you feel?*
> *Who is there with you and what are they doing?*
> *How do they feel?*

Are you ready to rise out of your RUT and go after the vision you have for your life? Decide today, right now, that you are ready and willing to make the necessary changes and start the important work needed for you to live the life you crave. Once you decide, commit to action, and start to craft your world.

Complete this exercise. It will give you an idea of what you need to do to craft a unique world where you can reconnect your purpose to your passion, thrive, and reach your goals. I suggest using a separate piece of paper so that you have plenty of room to brainstorm and write down your thoughts.

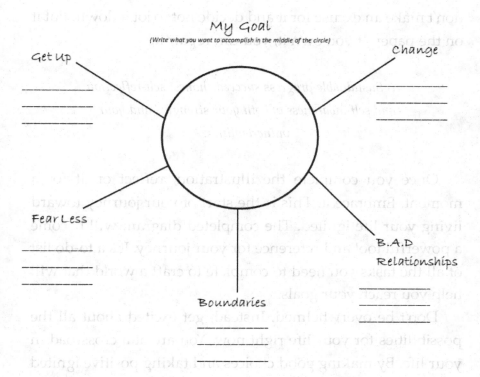

My Goal
(Write what you want to accomplish in the middle of the circle)

Get Up

Change

Fear Less

B.A.D
Relationships

Boundaries

Copy the illustration above on a separate piece of paper and write your goal in the center of the circle.

Each chapter of this book is represented on the illustration. Based on your takeaways from each chapter, write down specific things you need to do (Ignited Action Items) to reach your goal. Each action should be personal and within your control. Be honest with yourself as you write down your Ignited Action Items. Sometimes we change our perceptions to make reality a bit easier to bear when we don't like how the truth looks and feels. Don't do that here. Be real with yourself. Complete an honest appraisal of things you can improve for the purpose of being a better and more ignited you! If you reveal a problem, don't make an excuse for it and decide not to jot it down. Put it on the paper. If you own it, you can repair it.

Sustainable progress succeeds honest self-reflection and self-awareness of both your strengths and your vulnerabilities.

Once you complete the illustration, reflect on it for a moment. Embrace it. This is the start of your journey toward living your life ignited. The completed diagram will become a powerful tool and reference for your journey. It's a to-do list of all the tasks you need to complete to craft a world that will help you reach your goals.

Don't be overwhelmed. Instead, get excited about all the possibilities for your life right now. You are at a crossroad in your life. By making good choices and taking positive ignited actions toward living better and being a more focused and determined version of yourself, you will reach your goals and soar. Just like a firework, you will be unstoppable and powerful. This is your opportunity to put the pieces together and craft a world that is conducive to your dreams and works in tandem with the vision you have for your life. You have all the answers right here. And now that you know better, you have a personal responsibility to yourself to do better. It's time to put the concepts and ideas from this book, and all the others you've read, into action and begin to craft your world.

Life is not about finding yourself. Life is about creating yourself.
-Lolly Daskal

From this point forward, what happened in the past is in the past. Past mistakes are history. Shame and guilt stop here. They are not part of the world you are going to craft for yourself. Your past taught you lessons that made you stronger and wiser for the journey you are about to embark upon. In this new world, you will ignite your inner fuse and begin to live your life ignited. You will stand taller than ever before. You will lift yourself by dropping the baggage you've been carrying around all this time. You will no longer put your dreams and goals on pause. In the world you craft, you will eliminate BAD relationships and dream blockers. You will protect your world and define boundaries that must be respected by all those in your world. You will do this by respecting yourself enough to follow your dreams, reach for excellence, and not let anyone or anything deter you from your purpose.

Craft a world that attracts growth and progress. You have creative control of your life. The most important advice I can give you as you craft your world is to be authentic at all times. Crafting your world is not about gaining acceptance from others. Crafting your world is all about being happy with yourself and setting yourself up for success. Of course, there will be challenges and obstacles along the way—that's called life. Life doesn't always care about your plans, your passion, or your purpose, but allows strong foundation, rooted in your purpose, will help you navigate a bit easier when life gives you plot twists and unexpected turns.

> True happiness comes from the joy of deeds
> well done, the zest of creating things new.
> - Antoine de Saint-Exupery

When you craft your world, you also send a message to everyone who is watching: You put the world on notice that you are fired up, ignited, and ready for success. Let the world know you are a person with passion who is living on purpose, for your purpose, with a mission to pursue your goals and dreams. Let the world know you will not let anything stand between you and success. When you craft your world, you make a powerful statement that others have to honor. There will be some people and things that will naturally detach themselves from the world you craft because they are not attracted to it or they will no longer be a good fit in your life. Even better than being unattractive to dream blockers, is that you will begin to attract like-minded people with similar interests and journeys. This is exciting because a journey is always better when traveled with compatible people who believe in your goals and dreams and want to help you achieve them.

If you don't design your own life plan, chances are
you'll fall into someone else's plan. And guess what they
have planned for you? Not much.
- Jim Rohn

A few years ago, I decided to craft a world where I did not spend so much time consumed by unproductive activities. I evaluated friendships and pastimes. I saw the areas of my life where I needed to improve - and I did. I lost a few friends and acquaintances along the way -some I miss more than others. But that's okay because soon after I started losing old friends, I started making new ones. These new friends were motivated, successful, and overall good people. I didn't go out looking for new friendships. I didn't push myself on people. The friendships just happened. My new attitude was contagious to other ignited spirits, and as I met new people, they were able to sense the good energy bouncing off of me. I crafted a world that naturally invited like-minded people and things to my life.

Don't be afraid to own your truth and craft your world based on the authentic you – not the one you pretend to be around others. Make a statement to friends, family, coworkers, neighbors, and everyone around you that you have lit your inner fuse. Command respect for your goals and dreams by creating a world that will accept nothing less from anyone or anything. Take the necessary action to craft a world where you can shine, soar, and reach your goals. Ignite your inner fuse and use the to-do list you created in this chapter to start crafting your world today.

ENJOY THE JOURNEY

Enjoy the journey, hurry not toward its end, but take
each moment as it comes ... one day at a time.
-Author Unknown

ADULT PAINTING PARTIES HAVE BECOME a trend in recent years. I've gone to a few, and I've had a good time at each party. You go to a nice restaurant or a really cool art studio with friends (or other fun people), grab some paint and brushes and a good glass of wine, and sit in front of a blank canvas. When the host says go, you get to work on your masterpiece. There is always a master painting on display. The goal of the painting-wine-drinking party is to recreate the master painting on your canvas.

Most of the partygoers look at the master painting and say, "There is no way mine is going to look like that."

Despite some doubt, you sip your wine, laugh with friends, and do your best to replicate the master painting on your canvas. When the final brush stroke is complete and the paintbrushes are put down, everyone is shocked and amazed that their paintings have actually turned out pretty well. In a lot of cases, they are just as good, if not better, than the master painting. They created a beautiful painting—exceeding their expectations—and they had loads of fun in the process.

If laughter and wine were not in the mix, the painting process would not have been as fun. You have to approach your journey to living your life ignited in the same way. Your life is a blank canvas; with good company, a little instruction (this book), and a merry spirit, you can create your masterpiece, make your vision for your life a reality, and have an awesomely enjoyable time along the way.

Making life-changing decisions and working hard to live your life ignited is a serious process, but it should be a gratifying and rewarding experience too. Rediscovering, redefining, and refining who you are for the purpose of what you will become will be one of the most amazing times of your life. You have to embrace this journey as an exciting time where phenomenal things are happening. Don't look at it as stressful or painful work. Just as with other crafting projects, some elements are exhausting and tedious, but there should be moments where you smile, enjoy the project, and have a little fun.

Some people are miserable all the time because they miss opportunities to smile and enjoy the beauty of their journeys. We already know that change can be difficult, and along your journey to living a life ignited, you are definitely going to be challenged, frustrated, or ready to give up. But in the midst of

73

it all, there will be reasons to revel in precious moments. Your life is changing for the better – and that alone is a reason to feel good and smile.

When you plant a seed, you don't go outside the next day and frown at it because it's not blooming yet. Instead, you water it and nurture it. Every time you see a new stem, leaf, or bloom, you feel a sense of pride and delight because you know that the little seed is responding to your care. It is growing into something beautiful—one day at a time. Your journey is like that seed. You may not be where you want to be, but you are nowhere near where you used to be. When you see a stem sprout or tiny buds forming as you experience growth on your journey, take a moment to smile and get excited. And stay excited. Celebrate tiny milestones. Each small win brings you one step closer to reaching your big goals.

Throughout the growth process, make the best of what you have. Even in seasons of sacrifice or lack, pursue your purpose with joy and expectation. Embrace the blessings you have and be grateful and joyful along the way. As you work toward living your life ignited, have faith that your season of prosperity will come.

I just enjoy life now. I just enjoy every morning
I get to wake up.
- Nas

There was a period of time when my husband, Arnez, and I were broke - we had no money in the bank and no money in our pockets. We were young and just starting out. We were used to being broke. We both grew up broke and figured that this was just how it was – for now until were able to start laying our financial foundation. There was this one particular time when, after paying as many bills as possible for the month, all we had left was $36. We had to share that $36. He needed gas money for the week and I needed a transit pass to ride the bus and train to work every day. We also needed groceries, but they were going to have to wait until one of our next paydays. We had no money for food as we sat in our kitchen and wondered what we were going to eat one night. Arnez went over to the pantry, opened the door, and stared as if his hazel eyes were magical and going to make food appear.

There was no magic that day. The cupboards were bare. There was not much to work with; peanut butter, tuna fish, and stale cereal. We also had a box of penne pasta, half a bag of flour, and a bottle of red wine that someone gave us as a housewarming gift.

Arnez grabbed the pasta, flour, and wine and said, "I think I can do something with this." He grabbed a saucepan out of the cabinet and got to work. He heated the saucepan and poured in half the wine. When the wine started to bubble, he added flour to make gravy. In a separate pot, he boiled the pasta. When it was done cooking, he drained it and added it to the gravy. He added a few dry spices to the saucepan—and viola! - there was dinner! And it was good, too. He worked magic in the kitchen that night. We ate that pasta for three days—for almost every meal—until we were able to afford a trip to the supermarket.

It was the best meal we ever ate together. The pasta was delicious and it held us over until we were able to buy food for the pantry again. That pasta dish reminded us to be humble and grateful for what we did have. We struggled financially during that time, but our love, happiness, and gratitude was never compromised by the struggle. Those hardships created the foundation upon which we still stand on strong today. Without those experiences, our relationship would not be as fortified as it is today.

> *Life is 10 percent what happens to you and 90*
> *percent how you react to it.*
> *- Charles R. Swindoll*

Life would have been more difficult if we chose to feel sorry for ourselves and be mad and miserable because we didn't have enough money to do basic things. It would've been a crappy journey if we weren't hopeful, prayerful, and faithful. Having a positive outlook on life helped us make it through the hard times.

When I was a teenager, someone told me I was the most bougie poor person they'd ever met. They didn't quite understand how I could hold my head up so high and be so confident when I lived in a house with no hot water and in a home where we struggled to survive in the midst of alcohol abuse, drug abuse, and constant family chaos. He was one of those mediocre, unignited people that failed to understand that I focused my attention and energy on the person I was working to be. I did not let "temporary" conditions discourage me. I remember saying, "It's all how you look at the journey and operate along the way." Even though my home and my environment were not always conducive to success and yes, there was always chaos, cursing, and drama, I still had plenty of reasons to smile.

> *Nothing is impossible, the word itself says*
> *"I'm possible"!*
> *- Audrey Hepburn*

With the demands of everyday life, it's easy to get overwhelmed and discouraged with all that is required of you in the pursuit of your purpose. Enjoying the journey, however, cannot get lost or tossed aside as something you'll do if time allows or if you feel like it.

You have to make time for joy.

Enjoying your journey is mandatory for living your life ignited. You must learn to appreciate your path, applaud yourself as you reach milestones, and savor the sweet nectar of success as the seeds you've sown begin to bloom and blossom. Add these four ingredients to the mix of your daily life so you can begin to enjoy your journey toward your life ignited.

- pacing
- peace
- playing
- praying

Pacing

Some people take the quick-fix, get-rich-quick, lose-twenty-pounds-in-two-weeks approach to reaching their goals. However, there is no sustainability when you reach your goals that way—if you even reach your goals in the first place. Do you know anyone who lost weight by following a quick-fix fad diet? I do. I am one of those people. Did the person put that weight back on—plus a few extra pounds? I met my weight goals quickly, but there was no savoring the success. Shortly after losing the weight, I gained back the eleven pounds I lost— and I packed on another five pounds within six months. Your goal is not to be the Energizer Bunny of success and prosperity. You are not the Flo-Jo or Lance Armstrong of living your life ignited. This is not a race. This is a journey. Like a marathon, it requires you to pace yourself, take your time, and take care of yourself along the way.

Pacing requires patience. Don't be in such a hurry that you forget to take your time and calculate your steps. Enjoy God's beauty in your life - watch it unfold and manifest itself as you reach milestones and get closer to fulfilling your dreams and reaching your goals.

Even now, when I start to get a little impatient, I look around and think about how far I've come. I have grown so much and can see clearly how awesome God has been in my life.

They that wait on the Lord shall renew their strength
they shall mount up on wings like eagles they shall walk
and not faint
- Isaiah 40:31

Ignite your inner fuse and keep moving forward in expectation and anticipation of incredible things to come. Pace yourself and enjoy your journey - and the view along your way.

Peace

Peace allows you to accept your past and live in your present. If you did something in your past that you're ashamed of and that shame has you in bondage today, you have to let those feelings go. Search deep within yourself to find peace in knowing you made the mistake, you were delivered from that mess, and you are a better person today. You are stronger than you have ever been. Because you know where you are going, you can stand tall and proud. You can be at peace because your past no longer defines you or holds you hostage.

You should feel beautiful and you should feel safe.
What you surround yourself with should bring you peace
of mind and peace of spirit.
- Stacy London

Peace, your mind and spirit's contentment, also gives you to the ability to be calm when you should be freaking out. It allows you to chill in chaos. When you're calm, you can think clearly and make good decisions. When you are at peace, it's easier to smell the roses and see all the wonderful things around you. When you have peace, people look at you and wonder how the heck you are so calm when things around you appear to be such a mess. While they may not understand your low-key demeanor, you know it is simply the peace within you. You've been through fires and storms in the past, and you're still standing. This journey will have its fair share of obstacles and tests, but knowing the strength, courage, and determination that brought you through previous challenges will sustain you as you ignite your inner fuse and travel toward living a life ignited. You can go forward in peace because you already know there will be a rainbow after your rainstorm.

Playing

As you journey toward living your life ignited, you have to play. If you don't, you will burn out quickly. Play means having fun, enjoying a moment, or simply rejuvenating and relaxing. Playtime is important to living a life ignited because you need time to release stress, tension, and frustration. You are pouring your total self into this journey, but n doing so, you cannot forget the importance of lifting your head up, letting your hair down, and having a little fun every now and then.

My husband started his contracting business with $9,000 in 2005. He purchased a work van for $8,000 and a few tools. He started working as a handyman, doing small projects for people we knew. With hard work and dedication to his vision, he grew his business into a very successful company that specializes in commercial and residential property rehabilitations – a big jump from being a handyman. I'm so proud of him. Remember, this is the same guy who was broke and making magical pasta meals for us when we were money-less. On one hand, I was proud of my husband, and on the other, I became annoyed with the lack of "play" in his life. He would come home after a long day of working at various job sites, hop on the computer, and work a few more hours. He was always working, and the lack of sleep made him grumpy and difficult to be around at times. I love him and appreciate him wanting to take care of us by working so hard, but his lack of work-life-fun harmony was affecting our family.

One night, I got so frustrated by his heavy mood and the not-so-positive energy he was giving off that I stormed into his office and yelled, "Why do you work so hard if you are not going to lift your head up, look around, and enjoy the great life we have. If this is what working hard gets you, then I don't want it." And then I stormed out the room.

He kept working, and I went about my evening. Eventually, I went to bed.

We never spoke specifically about my outburst, but a few weeks later, he came to me and said, "You're right. What's the point of it all if we don't enjoy it? I got your message. We should be enjoying our lives." He told me to plan a trip, and that's exactly what I did. We spent ten amazing days in Europe with our kids. We traveled to London, Paris, Pompeii, and Rome. The experiences we shared together, the laughs we had, and the memories we made are priceless; they will last a lifetime. And ever since he told me to plan that European vacation, he has purposely incorporated "play" time into his life. Each moment of play is a gift, and we take those opportunities to rejuvenate, recharge our batteries, and reinforce our love and connection to our family and to one another.

Today, just take time to smell the roses, enjoy those
little things about your life, your family, spouse, friends,
job. Forget about the thorns -the pains and problems they
cause you - and enjoy life.
- Bernard Kelvin Clive

As I was writing this book, I found myself glued to my computer - from the time I walked in from picking my kids up from school to the time I went to bed, which was often past midnight, I was in my office typing away. Once or twice, my son would see me walking from the kitchen back to my office and say, "Mom, do you want to watch TV with me?" Even though he would catch me when I was in a really creative space—with a lot of thoughts I needed to get down on paper—I would stop and redirect my attention to him. I would watch TV or play a game of Scrabble or Uno with him. Even though this book and its deadline were important to me, I had to remind myself not to neglect precious moments with my kids. I'm going to look up one day, and this little tween will be a young man whose last thought will be playing Scrabble or watching TV with me, so I have to cherish these moments now and make time for "play". A life ignited involves a harmony between working hard and having some fun in the process.

Life is short! Reach out and grab it while you have it!
Embrace all those little daily things! Take time to smell
the roses. Don't rush through life. Live one day at a time.
Stop worrying so much, it gets you no where. Accept
what will be! Let go of all those things that weigh you
down! Live, Love & Laugh.
- Suzie Pierce

Things can change in the blink of an eye. As you journey toward living your life ignited, have fun and make room for "play" time. Ignite your inner fuse, be entertained, take time for friends and things that bring you joy, and don't forget to celebrate wins, milestones, and the people you love along the way.

Praying

> Seek the Lord and his strength,
> seek his face continually.
> - 1 Chronicles 16:11

I believe in God and in the power of prayer. When I am weak and feeling overwhelmed, I pray. I share my feelings with God and ask him to continue to love me through the journey and show me the way. I ask God to reveal himself in my life so I know I am truly walking in purpose. When I look around at all I have—my health, a family, love, and support—I look up and thank Him. When I see beautiful clouds in a perfect blue sky, I have to look up and thank Him for being so amazing and miraculous. Every year in Spring, when my azalea bush blooms, I think of God's goodness and power. If he could do all these great things in the sky and on earth, I'm sure He can keep me safe as I travel on my journey, working hard to reach my goals.

I hope you look up at the heavens and admire God for all his wonder and all He is capable of doing in your life. When working to live a life ignited—and then working to sustain the lifestyle you desire—you need support. Family and friends can't always give you the support you need. Sometimes you need to close your eyes and pray to God that He continues to reveal your purpose and help you as you pursue it with passion.

When your spirit needs to be lifted or your fuse is starting to dim, I want you to pray this prayer. This is a prayer for living Your Life Ignited.

> Dear God,
> Thank you for life, health, and strength.
> Thank you for carrying me when I thought I was walking alone.
> Thank you for bringing me through tough times and ordering my steps to march toward a greater purpose for my life.
> God, when I look to you, I am radiant (Psalms 34:5).
> Today, I am asking with a sincere heart and an open mind that you bless me as I journey toward living my life ignited.
> I ask you to decrease what limits me so you may increase in me so I can go the distance of my journey and thrive in life.
> Let my fuse be ignited and my light shine so I may reach my goals.
> Guide my thoughts and actions so I do not lose sight of the purpose positioned on my life.
> Let my journey be a blessing to others and a vehicle for positive change in my life and in my community.
> Your Word says, "These things I have spoken unto you, that in me ye might have peace. In the world ye shall have tribulation: but be of good cheer; I have overcome the world" (John 16:33).

As I face challenges, obstacles, and difficult people and situations, speak strength, peace, and courage to me, God.

I'm claiming today that I am a life ignited.

I will pursue my passions with purpose.

I am more than enough.

I will not fail.

I am more than a conqueror.

I've already won.

I'm victorious, and you are worthy to be praised.

Keep me God and help me be the best version of me I can be.

Thank you for your love, blessings, and favor.

Amen.

EPILOGUE

YOU HAVE ALL YOU NEED within you to ignite your inner fuse and live your life ignited. I hope you understand that. Say it, now...

I have all I need within me to ignite my inner fuse
and live my life ignited.

***

I have all I need within me to ignite my inner fuse
and live my life ignited.

***

I have all I need within me to ignite my inner fuse
and live my life ignited.

***

JUST AS A FIREWORK IS made up of gunpowder, potassium nitrate, and an array of other chemicals that give it unstoppable power, you too have the ability to combine specific ingredients into your life that, once ignited, will allow you to propel yourself forward, maximize your potential, and live your best life.

You don't have to keep going through the motions every day and feeling unfulfilled. By applying the mind-sets and behaviors you have read in this book, you can light your inner fuse. Once ignited, you will emit an energy and radiance that will bring light to your darkness. You will be explosive and unstoppable. You will conquer your fears, crush obstacles, and reach your goals.

> *But as it is written, Eye has not seen, nor ear heard,*
> *neither have entered into the heart of man, the things*
> *which God has prepared for them that love him.*
> *- 1 Corinthians 2:9*

Once you start to live a life ignited, your family, friends, coworkers, and peers will notice. They will see the change in you as you begin to experience growth and prosperity. Your light will bring out the beauty in others, too. You will inspire them to get out of their comfort zones, break the chains of mediocrity, and go after their dreams. Success and purpose are contagious!

Living a life ignited is all about embracing the possibilities for your life and being the best version of you that you can be. I pray that book helps you feel reconnect to your purpose and your goals and gives you a renewed sense of passion and confidence. I pray that you stay motivated and inspired to do the action and craft the world you deserve, desire, and crave.

Say good-bye to your comfort zone. Move forward with your goals. Ignite your inner fuse and let it burn brightly with immense enthusiasm for what's to come. Follow your heart. Pursue your passion with purpose. Be relentless with your dreams and a be a total fanatic about your life!

Be Inspired.
Be Motivated.
Be A Life Ignited.
Rhonda

ABOUT THE AUTHOR

Fueled by faith and optimism as she pursues her purpose with passion, Rhonda Kinard is dedicated to helping others rise out of their rut, reconnect their passion to their purpose, and reach their goals so they can experience their appointed position of prosperity in their lives.

Along with being a zealous mom and wife, Rhonda Kinard is a certified life coach, author, professional speaker, and mentor. She is the owner of A Life Ignited, a personal and professional development services company that positively affects the lives of others by motivating and inspiring them to live their lives ignited.

With more than fifteen years of experience as an entrepreneur, real estate investor, IT professional, wife, and mother, she brings an extraordinarily rich combination of knowledge, skills, and insight to every aspect of her writing, coaching, and teaching.

Rhonda and her husband have been married for almost fourteen years. She has two amazing children who are gifts from God. She loves to travel and spend time with her family. She enjoys photography, cooking healthy meals, and relaxing at the spa.

Visit www.ALifeIgnited.com and connect with Rhonda and A Life Ignited via Facebook (A Life Ignited), Twitter (@ALifeIgnited), and Instagram (A Life Ignited).

REFLECTIONS

REFLECTIONS

REFLECTIONS

REFLECTIONS

_____
_____
_____
_____
_____
_____
_____
_____
_____
_____
_____
_____
_____
_____
_____
_____
_____
_____
_____
_____
_____
_____
_____
_____

REFLECTIONS

REFLECTIONS

Reflections

REFLECTIONS

REFLECTIONS

REFLECTIONS

Printed in the United States
By Bookmasters

Printed in the United States
By Bookmasters